MW01127148

SIX SECRETS
TO SUCCESS IN
HIGH SCHOOL AND COLLEGE

DR. DONALD L. WASS
DON WASS JR.
and
AMANDA ROSE RAY

BOOK PUBLISHERS NETWORK

Book Publishers Network
P.O. Box 2256
Bothell • WA • 98041
PH • 425-483-3040
www.bookpublishersnetwork.com

Copyright © 2011 by Dr. Donald L. Wass, Don Wass Jr., and
    Amanda Rose Ray

All rights reserved. No part of this book may be reproduced, stored
in, or introduced into a retrieval system, or transmitted in any form,
or by any means (electronic, mechanical, photocopying, recording,
or otherwise) without the prior written permission of the publisher.

10 9 8 7 6 5 4 3 2 1

Printed in the United States of America

LCCN 2011910382
ISBN10 1-935359-90-8
ISBN13 978-1-935359-90-6

Editor: Barbara Kindness
Cover Designer: Laura Zugzda
Typographer: Stephanie Martindale

Graphic clipart © 2011 truck © Am1969 | Dreamstime.com, secret © Lavitreiu
| Dreamstime.com, blimp © Tmorris9 | Dreamstime.com, billboard © Stephen
Sweet | Dreamstime.com, sign © Zbb952 | Dreamstime.com

In Memory of

HELEN WASS
and
NOLAN MOORE

Contents

PART FOUR: THE WAR IS ON

PART FIVE: GRIM REAPERS I HAVE KNOWN

Acknowledgements

To the memory of my beautiful and ever-patient wife, Helen: She graciously and repeatedly proofread every word of this manuscript. She is the light and love of my life, and has been at my side every step of the way. There was never a complaint, even when she shouldered most of the load during my travel/speaking days. She has always provided everything a husband would want. Helen is my model for goodness. To her I owe everything.

A very special acknowledgement to my deceased parents, William Jacob Wass and Rose R. Wass. They provided me with a strong ethical and moral foundation. Their love of music and indomitable drive to succeed spurred me on to reach for the highest goals. Most of the credit for what I have done belongs to them.

To my children: Ann Marie, Margaret Mary, Nancy, and Don Jr. They were each, in their unique way, a constant source of help, encouragement, and affection. They will always be my pride and joy.

A special ThankYou to my daughter Margaret Mary, who provided the first edit of the book's rough draft. She also performed much computer wizardry, which allowed us to put words on paper.

To my eleven grandchildren, especially Amanda Rose Ray and Stefani Orscheln, now in college and high school, respectively, for their reality checks; along with my "pseudoadopted" grandchild Ashley Hagensick, now in college, for her updated experience.

To Dr. Julie Miller, who was so exciting, supportive, and helpful. She willingly allowed me to paraphrase her idea-mapping material that will provide students with a method to improve memorization and increase creativity.

To each of you students reading this book: it is our fondest hope that the material will make your time in high school and college at least slightly more enjoyable and a great deal more rewarding.

Donald L. Wass

To my wife, Heather, for the time and undying support you provided me. To my children: Audrey, Donny, and Maxton—May you realize the path to success is grounded in education. To my mother, Helen, for your wisdom and love that kept me on track. To my father, Donald, for being a guiding force, mentor, and best friend.

Don Wass Jr.

To my mothers, fathers, sibling, and family–

Nancy, my mom, for reminding me to always give hope a chance to float, because "though beginnings are usually scary and endings are usually sad, it's the middle that counts the most."

Margaret, for never failing to be the best "mom she didn't have to be," lending support to any and all endeavors I might encounter.

Helen, my "Grammy," for teaching by example the value of strong faith, close family, true friends, and proper etiquette.

Alan, my dad, for sacrificing so much to ensure my utmost happiness while still managing to be a guiding force in my upbringing; for showing me how to be strong no matter what.

Acknowledgements

Don, my "Da," for giving me all the possible opportunities and tools necessary to find the secrets to a meaningful life.

J.B. and Ashley, for continually proving to me the importance of responsibility, selflessness, and a positive attitude.

To those friends who have come to be recognized as family, for supporting me at my worst, and pushing me to be my best.

I will spend forever thanking you all.

Amanda Rose Ray

Part One
DANGER ZONES

Part One Introduction
Warning! Danger Zones!

Basic Ground Rules for Success

Everywhere you go you may encounter signs conveying rules to be followed in order to avoid negative consequences. Most are as simple as 'Stop' or 'Keep Right,' but what each entails is much more complex, as they help you to steer clear of potentially drastic problems.

Likewise, four danger zones will critically affect your success in high school or college. Of course, they will be devastating to your future if you ignore them. However, they will be just as destructive if you execute them poorly! Look upon them as being four cornerstones on which you can rest your high school and college experiences: Planning, Foundation, Attitude, and Emotional Stability. You must follow the right signs in order to ensure your safety in these areas!

**Secret No. 1
Emotional
Stability**

Sign #1

Scenario:

A man was playing the violin at a corner in New York City when a tourist, camera around his neck, walked up and asked, "How do you get to Carnegie Hall?" The musician grinned in response as he simply remarked, "Practice, dude, practice." Though most of us would smirk at that reply, there was actually a great deal of insight offered. The tourist was simply asking for directions, while the violin player countered with the proposal of a plan.

Planning is one of the most basic ground rules for success, so it comes as no surprise that *poor* planning is probably the greatest danger zone to avoid. Imagine the rolls upon rolls of plans required to construct all of the buildings, houses, and vehicles surrounding you on a daily basis. A set of plans was necessary for electricity throughout all of these structures in order to include lights, electrical outlets, switches, and so forth. Likewise, plans were needed for the duct work used in heating, ventilation, and air-conditioning.

As a more universal example, think about your favorite show on television. Got it? Now think about how much planning goes into each episode before it is finally ready for viewers to enjoy. On a broader scale, each such program's run time has been carefully mapped out down to a matter of seconds, taking into account the length, amount, and placement of commercials. Taking it one step further, suppose you are watching a football program on that television; I guarantee that within all that apparent chaos on the field, coaching staffs have spent hours concocting game plans for their team's success. Thus, when you delve deep enough into the inner-workings of almost any creation, chances are you will uncover the immense and intense planning that enabled their existence!

Some occupations even have witty sayings or jokes that remind workers to strategize well. Carpenters warn you to, "Measure twice and cut once." Painters point out, "Don't paint yourself into a corner." Plumbers always remind us, "Water runs downhill; plan for it." Your occupation as a student also requires much strategizing. Choosing what classes to take, which schools to apply to, how you will maintain your study habits, and how you will balance school and extracurricular activities: These all require critical arrangement on your part! In reality, success doesn't just happen; you must have a carefully developed and executable plan.

It is never too early to start planning. For college, plans should begin early in high school, even though only a small number of students will have a clear idea of what their career choice will be. In the same vein, college students will most likely change their major. Don't see your high school choice as being set in concrete. Instead, recognize that you can't change a major until you have one.

Ways to plan ahead in high school:

➢ Begin early in high school by meeting periodically with your counselor to stay on track for graduation.

➢ Continue to take the SAT/ACT often to increase college options and scholarship opportunities.

➢ Certain supportive choices can be made in high school if students have at least a general idea of what they want to study in college.

　　º One example; Selecting a foreign language that you would enjoy learning puts you a step ahead for college, since most colleges require two years of a foreign language.

Preparation for each coming day and self-discipline at home prove to be definite "musts" for students even as early as middle school, as such habits carry on in later education and careers. As a student, the planning process is essential in preparing for tests, writing papers, creating résumés—all ultimately leading to graduation and beyond.

In this book, we will show you how to utilize such strategies for your educational purposes. In a later chapter on choosing course electives, you will learn how, through careful planning, those electives may prove extremely beneficial in helping you make critical career choices.

Remember, if you don't have a plan, you don't have a chance.

Sign #2

The foundation makes the structure! Your lifetime career finds

its footing in high school or possibly earlier. Knowledge is accumulated by building on what is already known; hence, psychologists often remark, "The best predictor of success in college is one's success in high school." This building process requires us to learn the basic information first. Using math as an example, we must first learn the numbers and nomenclature. Then we are taught the signs that explain how to manipulate the numbers. Next, we learn basic relationships. Each step takes us to broader applications. Therefore, we can reasonably deduce that when a student receives an excellent foundation for a subject area in high school, the most important step has been accomplished. In college, learning proceeds more rapidly and to a greater extent. The more you prepare for your career now, the greater the benefit later. The clearer your ultimate goal, the easier it will be to build up to it in college.

Tips on setting a good foundation:

➤ Talk to your high school counselor about your career likes and dislikes.

   ○ For instance, advanced math and science courses in high school may be a necessity for the curriculum you are planning in college. On the other hand, you may need only introductory math and science if you are more inclined to choose arts and literature in college.

➤ Think about what foreign language you will choose.

   ○ You will need at least two years of a foreign language if your ultimate goal is a PhD. Many college students spend a semester of study in Europe. Knowing the language, even a little, would be a tremendous help. Acquiring the basics for that language in high school will make the process less demanding in college.

All courses in college are more readily understood, and thus learned, if you possess a strong and lasting foundation in high school. Such a strategy will help your Grade Point Average (GPA) in college as well. Grades do count!

Remember, it's difficult to place a foundation under a structure that is already being built.

Sign #3

Attitude makes all the difference in the world; it is truly the driving force in life. Hence, our third major danger zone is an approach with the wrong attitude

Take this [1]reflection from Charles Swindoll:

> "Words can never adequately convey the incredible impact of our attitude toward life. The longer I live the more convinced I become that life is 10 percent what happens to us and 90 percent how we respond to it.
>
> I believe the single most significant decision I can make on a day-to-day basis is my choice of attitude. It is more important than my past, my education, my bankroll, my successes or failures, fame or pain, what other people think of me or say about me, my circumstances, or my position. Attitude keeps me going or cripples my progress. It alone fuels my fire or assaults my hope. When my attitudes are right, there's no barrier too high, no valley too deep, no dream too extreme, no challenge too great for me."

The critical aspect about our attitude is that life is truly 10 percent what happens to us, and 90 percent how we respond to it. *You* get to decide whether your attitude will be positive or

---

1   Charles R. Swindoll, Strengthening Your Grip, (Nashville, Tenn.: W. Publishing group, 1982), pp. 206-7. Used by permission of Insight for Living, Plano, Tex. 75026

negative! As a young psychologist, I observed that those who generally thought things would somehow work out and who looked at the situation from a positive point of view, tended to be much happier. Those who espoused a sour view of life or tended to be pessimistic about how things would turn out were often seen as examples of "self-fulfilling prophecy." They predicted that the effort would fail. "It won't work," they would mutter in instant defeat. With half-hearted effort, they brought the failure upon themselves. When this occurred, they would then only remark, "See, I told you it wouldn't work and it didn't," as if congratulating themselves. By the same token, those who exuded a positive outlook enjoyed a much more pleasant time waiting for things to happen. Likewise, it seemed that those who saw the positive side were predisposed to deal effectively with the outcomes that were more neutral rather than completely positive or negative. Since the balance of results tips clearly in a positive direction, one's decision to be positive should be a no-brainer, though it is more easily said than done. The question remains, does attitude make a difference?

Scenario:

The Notre Dame football team was playing a regular season game. During the first half, the opponents were pushing and pummeling Notre Dame all over the field. At the half, the Notre Dame players were behind closed doors in the locker room without their coach, Knute Rockne. After a few agonizing minutes of silence spent brooding over the way they had already given up the game, a loud knock on the door reverberated off the walls. As everyone glanced up inquisitively in that direction, Coach Rockne, in his booming voice, exclaimed, "Oh, excuse me, I thought this was the locker room for the Notre Dame football team." He closed the door and walked off confidently, knowing this comment would positively inspire his team to play with passion in the second half in order to prove their worth, rather than hand over the unfinished game in defeat. As you might have guessed, Notre Dame dominated in the second half and won the game by a long shot.

Keep in mind that attitude shall always be *your* choice, and ultimately it is your attitude that makes the difference.

Sign #4

As we go through life, each one of us will be faced with changes in our emotional stability. Some of them will be minor and are referred to as *emotional upheavals*. Others will be major and can be classified as *traumas*. In the material to follow, we will deal with these two classes.

Emotional upheavals include: a dispute with a friend lasting a few days, a car that continually has something inoperative, a bad test result, something of consequence that was stolen, and similar situations.

Emotional traumas are far more important and disturbing. Examples are: parents' divorce, a major accident with injuries, breaking up with a longtime boyfriend or girlfriend, death of a family member or close friend, destruction of one's home, or other such events.

All of the above occurrences will have varying effects on an individual's emotional well-being. Some people, faced with merely minor setbacks, will be able to assimilate them and bounce back to their normal mental state. Others react dramatically, experiencing trouble sleeping, finding themselves unable to pay attention to or comprehend situations, or just simply to stop caring. In effect, they shut down. More commonly, many tend to find themselves somewhere between these extremes. Instead of suggesting that one try to tough it out, we have found a method developed by Dr. James W. Pennebaker, a mind/body researcher, that has proved to be a big success after such incidents occur. Anyone can execute this stress-relieving process in four days, at any preferred place where complete privacy is able to be maintained.

By way of setting the stage, use your imagination for a few moments. Imagine that you have become emotionally distraught in response to a recent occurrence of one such major or minor upheaval. By coincidence, you have an exceptional friend, whose connection with you is so close that you have always been able to divulge to this individual your deepest emotional concerns. Formation of this strong bond developed out of the realization that this companion listened sympathetically, was understanding, supportive, and nonjudgmental. Your friend is constantly reflective of your thoughts, leading you to always feel relieved and somewhat restored after your discussions. In fact, the liberation from stress could be equivalent to six months in therapy, only without the bill that comes with it! Wouldn't it be marvelous if everyone had a friend like that? Well, as a matter of fact, each of us sure does! That friend is actually *you*. By journaling your deepest thoughts, you are utilizing strategies of Dr. Pennebaker's Expressive Therapy that are aimed at reaching these same results.

Dr. Pennebaker pioneered the process of Expressive Writing, which has brought about significant improvements in the lives of those who have experienced traumatic and/or emotional upheaval. A large number of other psychologists have replicated his research with equally effective results.

The following [2]directions for proper utilization of the Expressive Writing Technique have, with the permission of Dr. Pennebaker, been reprinted here:

Writing and Health: Some Practical Advice

Writing about emotional upheavals in our lives can improve physical and mental health. Although the scientific research surrounding the value of expressive writing is still in the early phases, there are some approaches to writing that have been found to be helpful. Keep in mind that there are probably a thousand ways to write that may prove beneficial to you personally. Think of these as rough guidelines, rather than truth:

> ➢ *When getting ready to write, find a time and place where you won't be disturbed. Ideally pick a time at the end of your work day or before you go to bed.*

> ➢ *Promise yourself that you will write for a minimum of 15 minutes a day for at least three or four consecutive days. Once you begin writing, write continuously.*

> ➢ *Don't worry about spelling or grammar. If you run out of things to write about, just repeat what you have already written.*

> ➢ *You can write longhand or you can enter your thoughts on a computer. If you are unable to write, you can also talk into a tape recorder.*

> ➢ *You can write about the same thing on all three to four days of writing, or you can write about something different each day. It is entirely up to you.*

---

2   Pennebaker, J. W. (2004) Writing to Heal: A Guided Journal for Recovering from Trauma and Emotional Upheaval. Oakland, CA: New Harbinger Press. Reprinted with permission.

What to write about:

⊠ *Something you are thinking or worrying about too much*

⊠ *Something that you are dreaming about*

⊠ *Something you feel is negatively affecting your life*

⊠ *Something you have been avoiding for days/weeks/years*

In our research, we generally give people the following instructions for writing:

Over the next few days, I want you to write about your deepest emotions and thoughts, about the most upsetting experience in your life. Really let go and explore your feelings and thoughts about it. In your writing, you might tie this experience to your childhood, your relationship with your parents, people you have loved or love now, or even your career.

How is this experience related to:

🖉 *Whom you would like to become?*

🖉 *Who you have been in the past?*

🖉 *Who you are now?*

Though many people have not had a single traumatic experience, all of us have had major conflicts or stressors in our lives; you can write about them as well. You can write about the same issue every day, or a series of different issues. With whatever you choose to write about, however, it remains critical that you really allow yourself to delve deep into your very deepest emotions and thoughts.

Warning:

Many people report that after writing, they occasionally feel somewhat sad or depressed. Like seeing a sad movie, such feelings typically recede within a couple of hours. If you find that you are getting extremely upset about a writing topic, simply stop writing or change topics.

What to do with your writing samples:

The writing is for you and for you only. The purpose is for you to be completely honest with *yourself*. When writing, furtively plan to throw away the transcription once you have finished. Whether you actually keep it or save it is really up to you.

Some people keep their samples and edit them. That is, they gradually change their writing from day-to-day. Others simply keep them and review the content over and over again to see how they have changed.

Here are some other options:

📁 Burn them.

📁 Erase them.

📁 Shred them.

📁 Flush them.

📁 Tear them into little pieces and—

- 📄 Toss them into the ocean
- 📄 Let the wind take them away
- 📄 Eat them (not recommended).

In Pennebaker's original research, he worked with two groups:

📖 Expressive Writing Group (1)

- ° wrote about a trauma or emotional upheaval

📖 Control Group (2)

- ✎ wrote about superficial matters

He found that the expressive writing group (1) had 43 percent fewer doctor visits than the control group (2), who wrote about innocuous topics. He and other researchers performed a large number of studies on expressive writing, where they concluded the beneficial effects included:

➢ enhanced immune functions

➢ lowering of pain

➢ less sleep disruption

➢ reduced stress

➢ lower blood pressure

Research with college students showed:

➢ higher grades

➢ enhanced quality of social life

➢ alleviation of anger

Current research, based upon Pennebaker's techniques, has broadened the scope of such writing exercises to include test anxiety. Multiple studies have indicated that students who take ten minutes immediately before an exam to write about their fears and worries— especially those pertaining to the upcoming exam— show improved performance in test scores. Such research, supported by the National Science Foundation, suggests that writing exercises relieve part of the brain's processing power from being overburdened by worries related to current activities. Test anxiety and uncertainties fill up space in a student's "working memory," which is used to process information pertinent to the task at hand. Simply writing for a short period of time about these concerns prior to an exam has been shown to free up this memory, leaving more brain power to concentrate on the exam itself, rather than on the worries surrounding it. Studies conducted on both high school and college levels consistently demonstrated that the students who utilized this technique performed better on exams than did those students who were still ridden with anxiety going into the test.

SIX SECRETS TO SUCCESS IN HIGH SCHOOL AND COLLEGE

From the research results cited above, it is clear that a great deal of relief results from expressive writing along with a significant impact on one's emotional stability. Finding your emotional stability is the most important sign to follow and follow well, as it governs how you act upon the other three.

So remember to KEEP RIGHT on the road to success by following and maintaining these steps efficiently!

Chapter summary:

1. Planning is at the forefront of all success.
2. A strong foundation provides the basis on which to build.
3. Positive attitude is the driving force.
4. Expressive writing can help stabilize your emotional health.

1

So Why Worry Anyway ?

When a used car is worth $400,000

Decisions, decisions…they are all that life seems to be made of. Basically it all comes down to choices. Think about it. Something as small as the color shirt you pick out in the morning may have an impact on someone somewhere. Say you pick the bright red shirt instead of the boring white one due to a sudden urge to change up your style. You jump in your car on your way to work and while driving, a man in another car takes a second glance. That second glance was the reason he did not stop at that intersection and ran into a minivan with a back seat full of kids and a soccer mom on their way to school. Their lives, and the lives of who knows how many, are now changed forever.

I know, it is a tad bit extreme, but it just goes to show how far decisions reach. In the end those tiny choices, such as the color shirt you wear, just cannot be determined as right or wrong because they are so numerous. However, those little choices you make can add up to your fulfillment in life and *that* is the important part!

When you walk down the aisle with your high school diploma, the first thing you probably think is, "Yes, I am finally out of here!" The question is, now that you are out of "here," where will you go next? The decisions that await you at that moment are just as important as those forthcoming after graduation from college. The wave of panic that comes next includes the questions:

○ Should I search for a job that will lead to a career?

○ Should I go to college to prepare for a career?

Let's opt for going to college, and leave the immediate job route for another book. Anyway, it is far more sensible to prepare for a career through higher education than to hope an entry level job, just out of high school, will lead to one.

Choices: Pros and Cons

1. *Brain/Brawn*
     The vitality of youth and the lure of an immediate pay-check may cause some to think twice about a job, as opposed to setting off for college and having to attend yet more classes, day in and day out. On come the nagging fears of going to college: Will I be accepted? Where can I get the money? Will I be able to successfully complete a college curriculum? What major would I even want to go with? Will I be so in debt once I graduate that earning my degree won't do any good?

     Leaving home is risky, unfamiliar, and for some not at all inviting. Compare that to staying in a nice, comfortable home occupying the room you have had forever, eating familiar home cooking, and socking away money for the future.

     For those who do not find the idea of college an amazing life experience that should never be missed out on, let's consider the cons next.

2. *Earning Possibility*
     Undoubtedly, the thought of money every two weeks from a steady job and purchases with the swipe of a credit card

make getting by in this world seem easy. However, exploring the chart on the next page, we see the earnings potential for the typical high school graduate verses a bachelor's degree, a master's degree, and a doctorate. A brief analysis of the data shows a positive relationship between salary potential and education. In other words, the more education you have, the more money you make.

HIGHER EDUCATION = HIGHER SALARY

Since most things, besides the ones deemed *priceless* on certain credit card commercials, actually do cost money, opportunities will arise in housing, travel, and other material possessions that can only be realized with salary potential.

This discussion is not to say that specific individuals with only a high school education may not strike it rich on, say, a random oil venture, or with the invention of the Hula-Hoop or coffee collars. It simply points out that the probability of success in ownership is greatly facilitated with higher education. In other words, you will have to get an education to make the money necessary for the lifestyle you wish to lead, whether it is having children, traveling, or even living on your own.

3. *Life Has More to Offer*
Beyond the concept of money, the experience of four or more years of college provides an unimaginable array of broadening experiences. For example, a college student with the slightest interest in music may choose to enroll in certain electives that allow for exposure to music in all its forms—instrumental, voice technique, composition, and so forth. Consequently, this student will also be endowed with countless chances to develop a hidden talent, along with others who provide support and encouragement.

If art and art forms are in your blood, you will find true experts to guide your budding interest into lifelong pursuits. Should you harbor an astounding knack for putting words and thoughts on paper, you will be among those who share that talent and recognize it in others. If the study of marine life and aeronautics or parapsychology is a secret dream of yours, kindred spirits are waiting to show you the way. College students are in a position to carefully nurture such gifts to a point of extreme success! The possibilities are endless!

Annual Earnings by Education Level

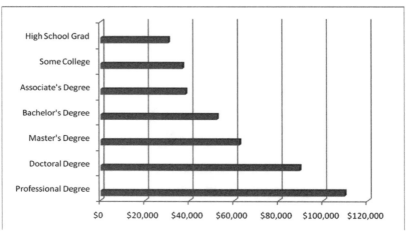

U.S. Census Bureau, Current Population Surveys, March 1998, 1999, 2000. Tabulations reflect the average annual earnings of full-time, year-round workers aged between 25 and 64 years.

Higher Education Facts:

> [3]Higher levels of education lead to higher earnings. Over a working life, the typical full-time, year-round worker with a four-year college degree earns over 60 percent more than a worker with only a high school diploma.

> Those with master's degrees earn almost twice as much per year, and those with professional degrees

---

3   Past facts from *Education Pays 2007*: The Benefits of Higher Education for Individuals and Society

earn almost three times as much as high school graduates earn over their working lives.

➢ Median lifetime earnings for the typical individual with some college but no degree are 19 percent higher than median lifetime earnings for high school grads with no college experience.

➢ The typical college grad who enrolls at age 18 and graduates in four years earns enough in 11 years not only to compensate for a loan equal to the full tuition at a public college, but also to make up for wages foregone while in college.

➢ College-educated workers are more likely to be offered pension plans. Among those to whom such plans are offered, college-degree holders are more likely to participate.

4. *A Person's Worth*

When you die, it is not likely that success will be measured by the size of your bank account, house, car, boat, or job. Rather, we suspect that the question others may ask will likely be in the vein of:

○ Did he/she help others?

○ Did he/she make a difference?

○ Did he/she leave the world a better place?

○ Was he/she a model to others?

○ Did he/she help the poor?

○ Did he/she create something of beauty?

○ Did he/she make us laugh?

○ Did he/she leave us a song?

○ Did he/she leave us with stories?

The answers to most of these questions have little or nothing to do with money. Such answers lie in the deep-seated desire and will on the part of an individual to reach his or her full potential in life, and to then share or give back the contributions received. Too often, we forget that others have helped us on our way, or that the gifts we each received at birth were not of our making. Leaving a legacy, like a positive answer to the questions above, is a fitting repayment.

5. *Looking Back*

Each of us probably knows hundreds of people, yet it is highly unlikely that one of them has said, "I wish I had <u>not</u> gone to college and gotten my degree." The more likely lament comes from those who say, "I wish I would have gone to college." When the time comes to make that decision, think carefully about all of the ramifications. If experience is lacking, discuss your issues with those who have advice to offer in such categories. Remember to talk to both those who have gone to college and those who have not. Extenuating circumstances may make the decision for you, but never give up on the dream.

6. *What You Have to Offer*

One TV ad ended with the words, "*A mind is a terrible thing to waste.*"

Just think of all the undiscovered talents that have gone to waste. The way to minimize the occurrence of such tragedy is to broaden one's environment so it may include exciting exposure to many of life's possibilities. Open yourself to life's experiences, if only to see whether or not a fit exists.

As it was once said, "*Try it, and you just may find that you like it!*"

Give yourself the gift of discovery. Listen for those congratulatory words, "I didn't know you had it in you." When you are sincere and persistent in your efforts, rarely will you be reduced to thinking the ever-so-true cliché: "If I only knew then what I know now."

7. When a Used Car is Worth $400,000
Imagine that a magnificent luxury car sells for $800,000. Having established that point, it is likewise reasonable to imagine that the same car with a few years of use could sell for $400,000 as a used car. Now change that car into a person—YOU. Look to turn yourself into a collector's item through attaining a higher level of education. In later life, your financial net worth will likely be far greater than those with lesser education. True, by the end of a college experience, one's youth has indubitably melted away. In its place, however, stands a certain maturity, and with that maturity comes success!

Chapter summary

1. At critical junctures in life, decisions are crucial.
2. Most things in life cost money, so get ready.
3. Some parts of life are priceless.
4. What will your legacy be?
5. Fulfill your dreams.
6. You are worth more than you think.

2

Choosing a Major Intelligently

No use in Running When on the Wrong Road

Case Study: Michael

Mike has just graduated from high school with above-average grades. During those blissful, adolescent days, he played tuba in the school band and got quite a kick out of it. He decides to major in band at college. After eight semesters of "oom-pa-pa, oom-pa-pa," Mike starts looking for a job, degree in hand. He is soon listed with all the employment agencies, but on nobody's payroll. Big business is just not interested in tuba players.

Case Study: Jamie

Jamie has a similar misadventure. She likes to paint, so she majored in art. Her artwork sold at the high school auctions every year and made a good amount of money. Now she can't get a job painting anything—not even fences!

Case Study: Freddie

Ditto with poor Fred. Since he was a little boy, he always envisioned himself as Sam Neill, (Doctor Grant) in *Jurassic Park*. After years of archaeology courses, Fred is digging ditches all right—but the only ruin he's apt to find is that of his own future.

What Michael, Jamie, and Freddie have in common is the fact that they all pulled the same vocational boner: They confused hobbies with careers. It is a cold, notable truth that most of the educated people in the world today are employed in business or industry. Very few successfully pursue occupations one would call "exciting": The big-time sports heroes and agents, Broadway stars, Hollywood idols, astronauts, explorers, and best-selling authors, to name a few.

Today's colleges and universities do a poor job of getting this simple fact across. Students are invited to drink from numerous fountains of knowledge, the contents of which are enticing, captivating, and exotic: paleontology, drama, radio and television, anthropology, music, astronomy…the list goes on. With little or no counseling about the true value of such degrees, the student goes dancing merrily down the yellow brick road to occupational disaster. In the cold light of practicality, "Great Expectations" soon become "The Impossible Dream."

Instead of falling victim to consequences similar to the ones these talented students failed to escape, be realistic when deciding on a major. Do so with thoughts of a lifelong career fixed firmly in mind, and clear away the pipe dreams. If you see yourself conducting the Boston Symphony, remember that literally thousands of other musicians, with Russian-sounding names, are in line for the job. Want to coach the Green Bay Packers? Join the crowd. Or maybe you aspire to produce five-star movies for the big screen, or become a famous actor or actress in such films; realistically, chances are you'll end up teaching drama at a small town junior high or directing a small theater group for $800 a month.

I'm not suggesting that these great expectations will never be realized. For a fortunate few, the impossible dream will come true. However, one should face such dreams with both feet firmly on the ground. The alternatives should be carefully weighed and the true values of the degree in question fully understood. Of course, you can most always use any degree to teach, if this idea appeals to you. On the other hand, if your ambition is to make money, you should understand that at the present time, the salary scale for teachers is relatively meager.

Of course, you may throw monetary consideration to the wind and proclaim, "Drama is my sole passion, and I'll devote my life to it no matter how poor I may become!" Fine! Years later, you may take some solace in the fact that you charted your own course. You were aware of the risks, but elected to forge ahead anyway. It's another thing to wake up years later with a copy of Stanislavski in one hand and a welfare check in the other, wondering, "When is the studio going to call?" That's really tragic!

This is not to say there is no place in the college curriculum for the "exotics." That is what electives are for—to enable you to wander briefly down those tortuous alleyways for which you hold a particular interest, before heading out on the highway full speed ahead toward your destination of graduation and beyond. You might even consider pursuing a minor in one of these exceptional subjects, if your more practical major is strong enough to support your professional needs.

Case Study: Rosalie

Rosie wishes to become a psychiatrist. In college, she majors in psychology, since her university does not offer a medical track. She also minors in German and Creative Writing, while taking American Sign Language as an elective. Now, most would wonder why she is wasting time and money taking unnecessary classes. Shouldn't she be taking Spanish, as it is a much more common language in the United States? Taking a closer look, we find that she actually put a lot of thought into her career when deciding upon such courses. She believes that with a minor in German she will be able to read such texts as those of Sigmund Freud, the "Father of Psychology," without any information being lost in translation. With her creative writing minor, not only will she be able to conduct research and studies her career will require, but will also be able to combine it all in writing, and perhaps even publish articles detailing her research. Having a background in sign language will give her another advantage, as many counselors and doctors come in contact with the impaired on a regular basis. If all this isn't enough, adding such factors to her résumé will benefit her greatly when she starts looking for a job, as each will enable her to stand out in a crowd!

The point is: Prepare yourself for your life's occupation first. You'll have the rest of your life to pursue Egyptology and, who knows, the income from your managerial position at Microsoft may well finance a summer pilgrimage to Cairo.

On the other hand, never put those pipe dreams out of your mind altogether. Many have been successful in turning what used to be a hobby into a profitable career or sideline. J.K. Rowling wrote the *Harry Potter* books in her spare time, and we've all heard those stories of Hollywood stars "discovered" while pumping gasoline, cutting hair, or waitressing. So write, invent, compose, act in the theater group if that's your dream—all the while working at some gainful employment you can enjoy! Someday, you just might discover a contract from Random House among those rejection notices, or some world-renowned director like Steven Spielberg or Ron Howard may turn up in the audience at the Pflugerville Community Theater.

Just remember to temper your dreams with practical, down-to-earth career plans in order to protect yourself and your family until that "Big Break" arrives.

Wipe Your Slate Clean

Don't start out with some preconceived notions about what you want to do in life. You'll have plenty of time to make up your mind and then go merrily down the road, oblivious to the facts. Until you succumb to that pitfall, why not map out another possible road to a successful career?

Gather the Facts

In order to give yourself as much help as possible, talk to two or three people whose opinions you value. Don't ask them to tell you what career you should choose, but rather ask for information about your strengths and areas where you might need improvement. Ask them what they think you are good at or would be good at, as well as areas they think you should avoid.

Be ready to ask questions about certain career fields where you have some interest. Example: "Do you think I'm detail-minded like most engineers?"

Listen between the lines while you jot down a quick note of what isn't mentioned, and ask those remaining questions after the discussion has concluded. Above all, don't alibi as you're getting information from them. The surest way to turn off this source of information is to argue with the person who is trying to do you a favor. It may not be what you want to hear, but take your medicine. You asked for it.

See Where Your Mind Says You Should Be

Most colleges and universities have a department that provides psychological testing services for students. You'll probably have to look for it, because few students have heard it exists. When it *does* come to light, common talk of this department among students most commonly includes some negative label like "Quack Shack," or a disparaging remark along the lines of, "Well that's where they send you when they think you're about to commit academic suicide!" Do not let such banter deter you. Utilization of such aid might just reward you with a first-class ticket to excellent professional opportunities, and you would then be the one laughing all the way to the bank behind a satisfying and successful career! The psychological services department can help you gather some pertinent facts by administering a battery of tests. Usually they include an intelligence test, a number of aptitude tests, a vocational inventory, and possibly a personality test. The intelligence test will give you some idea of what you could realistically expect to do purely from the mental horsepower side. The aptitude part will provide you with information specific to a particular area. An example would be the programmer aptitude test, which predicts your probability of success in the field of computer programming.

The two remaining types of tests—vocational and personality—are highly transparent or fakeable. For instance, unlike an intelligence test, the vocational survey may ask, "Would you rather, (1) sell tickets to the play, (2) act in the play, (3) be a part of the play director's staff?"

One can easily determine in advance which response correlates to what vocation. The same is true of most personality tests. So, the advice is to answer the questions in both tests with the utmost honesty, because the results are important to you.

In some vocational tests, the responses of the individual are simply compared with the responses of a large number of individuals already successfully employed in a particular field. The areas that match are presented as those in which the individual is likely to succeed since his or her likes and dislikes matched those of people already in that field.

Personality tests, on the other hand, allow a wide variety of interpretations. The validity of such interpretations resides more in the *individual* making the interpretation than the test used. Again, since the testing department is a university-sanctioned activity, it is reasonable to assume competent psychologists will make those interpretations.

Armed with the information gleaned from the testing process, you will then have further basis for talks with those who know you best. As you explain your test results to a family member, friend, or counselor, ask for their feelings concerning the accuracy of the interpretations. Send up more trial balloons on various career opportunities to get their impressions of how you might fit. Above all, keep clearly in mind the fact that ultimately the decision must be made by you. Only you can be responsible for the results. The above information can also be obtained from commercial enterprises such as AIMS (Aptitude Inventory Measurement System), where an even more comprehensive evaluation can be made, or online at www.aimstesting.org.

Interview Professionals

Let us assume now that you have narrowed the field to a few career possibilities. Another important step is to seek out one or two individuals who presently pursue each of the career areas in which you are interested. These interviews will prove vital. You will have an opportunity to learn what it is like to earn a living in that career, and receive in-depth details pertaining to a day in the life of a professional within the field. Again, prepare a list of questions. You may wish to ask questions that will help establish a specialty within the career field.

Game Time

Having amassed all that information, you are ready to decide. But our advice is to hold off for a while longer. "Sleep on it," as my grandmother always said. Forget about it for a couple of days. Give your subconscious mind a chance to sort through the data. Following that respite, go through all the facts again and make a decision. You'll find it much easier to make the decision if you keep in mind that there will always be time to change it should new significant data appear.

Learn to Love It? Easier Said...

Finally, just a word about the kids who struggle through school learning to be something they despise, just because someone else thinks it will be good for them. How many young men and women pursue law just because Daddy is a lawyer? How many choose to study accounting purely because Uncle Steve promised a position with the firm? There comes a day when they each face the awful realization that he or she hates law, or that Uncle Steve's accounting firm is not the only place of business in the world today.

Remember that your choice of a career is one of the most important decisions you will ever have to make; more important than which fraternity or sorority you will pledge, and possibly even more important than your choice of a marriage partner. Make this decision carefully! Be sure your vision is not obscured by childhood illusions of grandeur, and that you do so with all the available facts at hand. Finally, reserve the right to make that decision your own. Don't let Uncle Steve, Mom or Dad, or even your best friend, plan your life for you!!

You may eventually change your mind and even your major. Fear not! About one half of the college population changes majors at least once. If you find you're on the wrong track, make that change, even if it costs you an extra semester or two. It might well be the most crucial semester you will ever endure!

Chapter Summary:

1. Don't confuse a hobby with a career.

2. When deciding on a major, weigh all the facts: (a) How much can I expect to make? (b)Will I be happy in this work? (c) What are the job opportunities and where?

3. Talk to people who know you best.

4. Take advantage of psychological testing for careers.

5. Visit with one or two people presently working in the career you favor.

6. Know why you are pursuing a certain course of study, and make sure that the decision is your own.

7. Don't be afraid to make a change, even at the cost of additional time in school.

3

Apple Polishing for Fun and Profit

How to Win Friends and Influence Transcripts

Think the Studying Stops at Course Materials?

Better Think Again!

We all have a desire to be liked by everyone. Although many do not act as such, teachers and professors are no different. In the business world, it is said that people do business with people they like; the same goes for the educational universe. Although teachers and professors have little to do with those who sign up to take their courses, students have *everything* to do with whether their teachers or professors are fond of them, loathe them, or even notice them.

Throughout the eight critical years of life in high school and college— not to mention additional years

Secret No. 2 Study the Teacher or Professor

for graduate school or medical school, if so enrolled— the people you are associated with are divided into three key groups, separated as follows:

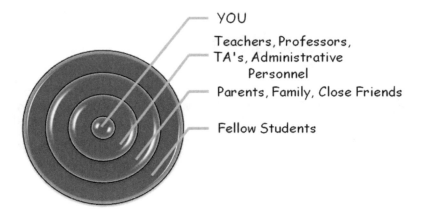

YOU

Teachers, Professors, TA's, Administrative Personnel

Parents, Family, Close Friends

Fellow Students

We will call this the School Bell Target Circle: The bull's-eye is, of course, you. Encircling you are your teachers and professors, teaching assistants, graders, and other school administrative personnel. Around them is a second group that consists of parents, other family relationships, and close friends. The outer circle represents your fellow-students.

POP QUIZ

Here's a hint: If you know one answer, you know them all!

1. Who teaches your educational courses?

2. Who evaluates the various course tests, quizzes, homework and class participation, and assigns a grade to each one?

3. Who determines your final course grade?

4. If a recommendation from an educational institution is required of you, who will provide one?

3: Apple Polishing for Fun and Profit

Do the words *Teachers and Professors* ring a bell? It sure does…. That is the sound of the School Bell Target Circle resonating in your head! If you answered those three words to each of these questions, then you aced it! Bravo!

This exercise is simply meant to show that the single most important influence to your future career is the closest group to the bull's-eye: Teachers and Professors.

Who is the second most significant influence to your future career? That's right! It is your parents, other relationships, and close friends. That, of course, leaves the third most prominent influence to be your fellow-students.

The data given up to this point follows logically that students who are seriously interested in their careers must primarily obtain and maintain the lively support of their teachers and professors. Only after this first goal is checked off the list should one begin to concentrate on the familial and student persuasions. Here's where the bell comes in.

Think back to elementary school. One of your biggest fears during school was getting in trouble, yes? Let's walk through a child's usual thought process concerning these matters:

Child makes a mistake –

Child is disciplined by Teacher, Principal, or another authority figure. –

Parents are notified –

Child is punished at home for what happened at school –

Child is embarrassed in front of or forbidden to play with other kids because of –

The child's initial mistake

And that, my friend, constructs one intense circle! Now I am sure this *does* ring a bell. However, I bet you never thought it would become a lesson on which the rest of your educational career relied! Allow me to connect the dots…. The prime target of the scenario mentioned is the child, now referred to in the School Bell Target Circle as YOU. The first figure you come in contact with, both as a child and in the circle, is the teacher or professor…surprise, surprise! The parents, family, and friends only come into play as runner-ups to this crucial confrontation. Hence, this chapter concentrates on number one—teachers/professors— because they are the most complicated and most critical to one's immediate career. Those interested can later extrapolate the major approaches to the remaining two groups, if you wish.

Strategies for Putting the Circle into Motion

The foremost strategy suggests that you take responsibility for bringing out the absolute best in each person with whom you study. Remember that golden rule: Treat others as you'd like to be treated? After all, teachers are people too! The following story should clarify this approach.

On the way to the West Coast to attend a family wedding, we stopped in Las Vegas for the evening. During casual conversation with our extremely outgoing cab driver, I mentioned that we had only one night to stay, and wondered whether he knew anything about the best show on the Strip. He answered, "The Wayne Newton Show," supporting his position by informing us that it was the most popular topic of conversation among customers departing from the Strip. I logged that information into my memory, but decided I would get a second opinion. Upon arrival at our hotel, I again explained our situation to the bellman and asked for his input. To my amazement, he suggested, "If you're only here for the night, you couldn't go wrong by seeing Wayne Newton." Well, that convinced me. We bought tickets at the information counter and grabbed another taxi, the Wayne Newton show our destination.

His performance remains fresh in my memory to this day. He sang a number of songs and then began to talk and joke around with the audience. Wayne asked, "How many of you are thrilled to be here?" About half the audience clapped (mostly women). "How many wish you were somewhere else but the other half dragged you here?" A decidedly greater number clapped and yelled. At that moment, I thought to myself, *Wrong Message!*

Wayne, being a professional, acted as if he didn't hear it. He went on with the show, playing every instrument on the stage as well as or better than the band members who primarily played them. He passionately sang the lyrics, danced as if no one was watching, and brought the audience to their feet. When the concert came to a close, the audience screamed and clapped until Wayne returned for an encore, exhibiting even more energy than before. The audience went wild when Wayne came out a second time, matching their enthusiasm. By that time, he had the audience in the palm of his hand and emerged a third time, exceeding everything already experienced. Finally, Wayne glanced at his watch and admitted, "Ladies and gentlemen, we have run way overtime. They're going to kill me, but you have been a magnificent audience and it was worth every minute. Have a great stay in Las Vegas! Thanks, to all of you!"

The show was over. I listened carefully to the exhilarated exchanges taking place all around us. "Best show we've seen since we've been here!" "Wayne Newton is a marvelous performer." "We've *got* to tell our friends to go see him."

As we were getting ready to leave, the servers began hastily clearing the tables for the late show. I conversed with the guy working at ours: "You people must be a little put out, since Wayne Newton ran over at our show." His reply was incredulous "Ran over? He usually does six to eight encores. He only did three tonight!" I was in utter disbelief; until it dawned on me….We did it to ourselves! The audience we took part in did not, by any means, bring out the best in Wayne Newton. We short-changed ourselves. Wayne got the same amount of money for doing the show with three, six, or nine encores. The fans, however, only got out of the experience what they put into it.

Soon after, I began progressively to reflect upon this occurrence. I ought to have been able to predict it. As a speaker, I have encountered many audiences. When an audience stimulated my energy with their own, I could perform my duties effortlessly, finding it so easy to converse with and relay stories to such a positive crowd. I enjoyed such instances immensely, and always seemed to remain thrilled long after the job was done.

Therein lies the key to drawing out the best qualities of your teachers. You can be reasonably sure that every teacher or professor lives for the chance to stare into the eyes of their students and find them dazzled with excitement. They want to know that you are paying attention and that you are taking notes, and they do look for that. If they pose a question, they want hands raised with an eagerness to answer. If they relay something that is supposed to be comical and everyone laughs, chances are that enjoyment will compel a brightened disposition on their part. When the students hang back after class, or come early to discuss the material covered in class, can you imagine how pleased their teacher or professor must be? The students who make their professor feel like a winner are the ones that win in the end!

In some colleges, more often than not, a T.A. (teaching assistant) evaluates the tests and issues a grade that will aid in determining the final grade. Consequently, what is being said about the professor applies in the same manner to the T.A. or the Grader.

Liking your professor psychologically inclines you to more readily learn and to retain what is taught. Conversely, not liking the professor predisposes you to learning and preserving less of what is taught. So, if you just cannot put up with a professor, the best suggestion is to switch to a class being taught by someone you can enjoy. If such a change is impossible, work diligently to remain neutral mentally toward the professor , thereby minimizing the subconscious handicap. Remember, the decision to like someone or something is your own. Be good to yourself. It's more fun that way!

Make It More Interesting by Showing Interest

There are countless ways to show interest in another. When you are genuine, the other person tends to reciprocate.

Example:

The next time you are in a restaurant, ask the waiter where he or she was born and, if appropriate, how his or her name should be pronounced. You'll be amazed how much better the service is!

Getting back to our professors, here are a few approaches. Students readily understand that it's necessary to attend high school or college in order to study the subjects that will prepare them for the career of their choice. What many do not understand, however, is that *studying the teacher or professor* is an integral part of that overall mission. Perhaps another story might help to clarify:

In graduate school, we had a professor by the name of Dr. Owen who taught labor law. He had been at the university for many years and was much loved by both students and other professors. I had planned on a minor in this particular area, so I decided to learn everything I possibly could about Dr. Owen. I staked out a seat in the front row, put my eyes on this man when he came into the room, and locked my attention on his every move and word, only momentarily pausing to take a quick note.

Since I *wanted* to learn it all, it was simple to pay attention and internalize the information. Discussion sessions were welcomed because they were an opportunity to test one's understanding of the subject matter. The information also provided topics for further reference at the end of class, before the next class, and at an occasional appointment with Dr. Owen during office hours. After some time, I could anticipate what would come next. The material was quite easy to remember, and it was enjoyable. I recall the times when Dr. Owen announced that there would be a test the following class, and I was excited about the chance to see how I was really doing. Some might roll their eyes or laugh at this, but when the test papers were returned, it never came as a surprise to see an A at the top. As Doc announced when the final test would be given, to me this was just another opportunity to shine. Immediately after class, a close friend of mine came up and whispered, "What is he going to ask on the test?"

I said, "How would *I* know?"

He replied, "I don't know how you do it, but somehow you come up with the questions."

Finally, I reasoned, "Well, I'm not sure, but he will probably ask a question on..." such and such. "Also, he was pretty excited when he talked about that labor strike."

Sure enough, when the final was placed before us, those exact topics I had described a few days earlier accounted for most of it. Just goes to show how becoming a student of both the professor *and* the subject, rather than just the subject, enables one to anticipate the course of the Course, so to speak.

Those who have seen the movie *Patton* may recall when, after Patton had outmaneuvered German General Rommel, he yells out into the field, "I read your book, you blankety-blank!" In other words, he was saying, "I studied you as a person, Rommel, so I was able to anticipate your every move and *that's* why I won!"

So, when you enroll in a course, make an effort to meet with the professor before the first class or soon thereafter. Ask about the class syllabus. Try to delve into what the professor likes and dislikes about this subject. Inquire about recommended reading material that would provide a more comprehensive exposure to the subject matter. Ask questions concerning how he or she tests class progress. For example, will essay or objective items be used in the tests, or will a teaching assistant be present? Determine what title, Dr. or Professor, is preferred. This shows consideration and respect!

First day

On the first day of class, make sure to arrive early to stake out a front row seat on either side of the room. Choosing one in the middle may require you to move your head from side to side all class, if the professor wanders around the room. The biggest compliment you can give a professor is to put your eyes on him or her and not take them off except to write a note about the presentation. Most, not all, professors like to have the class participate in discussion of the material. Without fail, join in the discussion, being mindful of two concerns:

1. Do not monopolize the time.
2. Do not initiate a heated discussion for sake of argument. Rather, play with the discussion, smile when you make a point, and be mindful that the professor wants to have a good time too.

Assignments

Pay particular attention to assignments. Take notes on what has to be covered in a paper, how long it must be, the date and time it must be submitted, the format of the presentation, and the elements that must be included. At some later date, if there is a question, the professor can gather from your notes that you had at least attempted to do it right instead of merely trying to remember it.

Attendant materials

Between class discussions on a particular topic, search for supporting material on the subject, especially something that appears in current events. It would be wise to ask others to keep an eye open for such material as well. Little can be of more interest to a professor than to have one of his or her students add to the understanding of what is being presented.

Study the professor in a holistic way

Your purpose as a student is naturally to study the courses being presented. Equally imperative, however, is the fact that you must become a student of the teacher or professor in a more complete way. Admittedly, there is precious little time to accomplish what is being required by the course. In one sense, though, you are ensuring a successful outcome by remembering and acting upon this tip. Only three prime time periods are available for a study of the instructor to be accomplished: Before class, right after the class ends, or at an appointed time during his or her office hours. This last option is most generally recommended because you are meeting on the professor's home territory. By way of preparation, determine some point or concept you wish to have clarified. Following that, be observant and listen for valuable information. Look around the office for pictures that will give you a clue to the professor's family or hobbies. If golf memorabilia are displayed, you can ask about his or her handicap or favorite course to play. If you see a picture of a spouse and/or children, ask about them. Background music might be playing when you enter. Determine the genre and state your similar tastes. Trophies are a dead giveaway, and you must inquire about them.

Occasionally, during class the professor might refer to how something relates to sports car driving, for instance, or some other activity. Make a note of such facts because they represent the professor's interests.

Try to be helpful in, before, or after class. Offer to organize any activity that might come up in the class. In general, you should strive to use the information you gather to better predict the professor's biases or preferences. Without being a sycophant, slant your written material to support what the professor prefers, and avoid what he or she obviously does not prefer.

During your efforts to study the professor, do what is necessary to find out his or her birthday and/or other celebratory occasions. If you are fortunate enough to have one of those dates fall during a normal class session, rally the troops to get a cake and celebrate. Learn everything you can about the professor. It may, in some way, be highly valuable to your ultimate success.

Chapter Summary

1. Decide to like your teacher or professor. Psychologically, it prepares you to learn and retain more.

2. Show interest by your behavior.

3. Sit in a front row seat, establish eye contact, and participate.

4. Complete assignments; look for attendant material.

5. Study the professor.

4

Meet Joe College

Flunking Out of School on the Buddy System

You just received a letter from the College Board informing you that due to your poor academic performance your enrollment in the university has been suspended. You have now formally been accepted into the faux-Greek society of Omicron Lambda Kappa, Oha Lotta Krappa or OLK for short. What is the next step?

Before we review your options, let's look at what put you in this unfortunate, but sometimes enriching, position. I like to call it the Buddy System!

College is a time for both self-exploration and academics. This is a time when a person not only makes choices and decisions *for* himself or herself, but *by* himself or herself as well. It may be the first time that someone has been, as we say, "on their own," and he or she quite possibly is not used to the responsibility of having control and making the best decisions.

When students enter the social and academic scene in college, you can be assured they will *not* know the motivations of the people around them and might not even be in touch with their own incentives for attending. While most are in college to learn, some are in it for the adventure, some wish to excel further in the world of sports, some submit to pressures from family tradition or societal status and, quite frankly, some are in it for the four P's: Parties, Pranks, Pickups, and Puke-and-Rallys (headed toward a dead end). It is your choice.

Case Study: James

James was a guy who made it a point not to purchase the required texts and computer software for a number of classes, and not because he couldn't afford them. He just felt that classes were getting in the way of college, and money spent on them could be put to way better use. Therefore, he figured if he absolutely had to, he could read one of his classmate's books and retain the information until the final exam. Since it was still possible to pass the class with a zero percent (0%) in the online quiz column, he just decided to skip those sections. He had plenty of free time, and would never fail to kill the curve in any class. He was always angling for a relief Buddy to hang out with and take the edge off, even if it meant cutting classes, reducing what little study time he had set aside, or losing the alone time that was usually spent giving himself a much-needed reality check.

Case Study: Brad

Bradley felt that summer vacation was way too short and chose to skip the first week of classes. He convinced his roommates and friends to do the same simply by offering to supply the keg and bring the girls for a week of festivities to end the summer with a bang. Besides, he thought, the only reason to go to the first week of classes was to get the syllabus. The professors couldn't possibly teach anything important in those first couple of classes because people were adding and dropping sessions like crazy before the deadline when they would be stuck with their choices!

Case Study: Ken

Ken didn't have time for study and classes due to the time he needed to spend working out, practicing, or bonding and formulating game plans with his teammates.

Case Study: Charles

Charlie was acting like a flower child, breaking away from his parents on a quest for self-actualization. He thought that professors spent their time teaching the people of the world the wrong ideas and ways of life. Therefore, he did what seemed the honorable thing and did not waste his time listening to them. Of course, or should I say, lacking a course syllabus, Charlie devoted long hours to leading environmentalist activities and preaching his Save-the-World, Hug-A-Tree values to the rest of the students on campus. His down time was spent philosophizing with his friends in a relaxed environment. Basically, Charlie spent his college years reliving Woodstock.

What do all these guys have to do with *you* when you have no idea even who they are? The point here is, you never know the motivational drives of the people you will meet in college, or later out there in the real world. Therefore, it is important to grasp your own values and hold on tightly in order to make it tough for people like James, Brad, Ken, and Charlie to bring your guard down, causing you to stray from your own morals.

How about a little personal experience:

"Chris, let's run over to Devaney's, grab a couple pitchers, and work on our beer-pong shots before Econ class. It'll make that old snore of a teacher less boring and get us ready to rule the table at tonight's party!"

It happens to all of us at some point. Personally, I had it in my head that I was just doing what I was supposed to do as a student, living the college life to the fullest...until that old snore of a professor we assumed would never know the difference rhetorically asked, "Who won the game?" as we stalked in laughing and half-stumbled on everyone else's feet trying to make it to our seats. After such a close call with the OLK, you bet I chose never to head off campus in between Psych and Econ again!

Now answer truthfully: Would you have naturally skipped class, or was that an example of the buddy system rearing its ugly head?

I am in no way suggesting you must bury your head in the books and not look up for four years. However, some students do fail in achieving a college education because of the influences exerted by the buddy system. College is a very exciting time, but hopefully you will not let that go to your head and find your name residing on the OLK system membership roster. Sometimes, academic goals and the buddy system can collide and create a landslide of events that may quite possibly lead to Expulsion by Buddy or EBB, for short.

There is no doubt that you have already accomplished a number of goals through your high school studies, and even through your Frosh or even Junior years in college, if that is the case. Getting through high school with a diploma or getting into a college at all are fantastic achievements in themselves! Each puts you in a position to achieve success in attaining the greater goals you have determined for yourself, such as a career or a degree. You made it, Baby! Why throw it away? Why join the EBB or OLK crowd? Now, some of you are undoubtedly thinking, "I am accepted in college, I am focused, I want to make it happen," and that is the attitude you must not only start with, but also be sure to sustain! You ought to constantly strive to be the cautious, conscious, "on-top-of-it" component of the Buddy System. Abiding by this rule will assure your protection against the dark, beer-stained pit of, perhaps, no return.

WHOOPS...

All right, so you became chairman of OLK. Oops, time to take a look at your options. Hey, let's face it; some just are not cut out for college, others need a wakeup call, and many just need a good swift kick in the rear! You have been dealt your cards and now you have to make the best of your hand. So what are your options? Despite what most might believe when caught in the throes of OLK, there are in fact a number of options to explore.

1. *Community College*
    Since the community college philosophy postulates that virtually everyone can benefit from a college education, there are minimal entrance requirements. Basically, there is just one, and that is high school graduation. As we say in Texas, YEE HAW. But don't let this fool you! A good number of Buddies await you in the community college system too who would love to help restore your membership in OLK. The purpose of many community colleges is to provide students with their first two years of collegiate academic study. Common benefits include:

❖ the ability to acquire a better GPA than the one you ended high school with, in preparation to attend a university

❖ an alternative when denied acceptance from a university

❖ a much more affordable way to stay in the educational system while acquiring the money to attend a university.

In your case, though, community college presents a way to jump-start the GPA that dive-bombed at your "weekend in college" (thanks, Steely Dan). Mike, one of my buddies, had a full-ride scholarship, but after his frosh year was inducted into the OLK system. The college advised him that unless he improved his GPA at another institution of higher learning, he would lose his scholarship for the remaining three years. You can bet that he went over to the nearest CC and took four classes that would boost his GPA to a point that enabled him to continue his education on full scholarship at his original college.

As previously mentioned, community colleges also serve as a launching pad for those who have not decided which college to attend, or who may have been caught off guard with the admissions process to a university. Community College is a wonderful resource, although many fail to notice this when the idea of attending such a school arises. Students interested in obtaining a bachelor's degree, for example, benefit from CC's transfer program of credit to universities. Undergraduates are able to take the first two years of their bachelor degree program at their community college and then transfer to the four-year university of their choice, saving a significant amount of time and money. Many students use CC's to their advantage during their first two years of study by taking the same courses found in universities while enjoying the extra incentives of:

- ❖ smaller classes
- ❖ more academic assistance
- ❖ much lower tuition

2. *Military: Army, Navy, Air Force, Marine Corps, Coast Guard*
The perfect university has high academic standards, moral discipline, free tuition, free meals, and free room and board. Impossible? Nope. The US military services allow for checks across the board. With a high school diploma, there are a number of ways to succeed in the military: mechanical, administrative, electronics, and general. The GI bill pays for most college expenses. Room

and board and personal trainers are complimentary from the government. What a wonderful way to escape the OLK crowd and get in great shape! Not only would you be increasing your chances of success in the future by taking this route, but you also would receive the public's admiration., The military is not for everyone, however. Forty percent of recruits who enlist in the military today will not complete their full term of service. Many discharges are due to reasons beyond the recruit's control, such as medical problems that develop after joining the military. However, a significant number of involuntary discharges imposed on first-term recruits are the result of a simple lack of motivation—these students discovered that the military wasn't what they thought it was going to be. Thus, they found themselves back where they started in the OLK system.

3. *Trade School*
A number of trade schools in the United States offer a wide array of vocational training in different trades and skills, and they are a great escape from the OLK. Usually, attendance at a trade school occurs when one serves an apprenticeship or wishes to obtain training in a specific area. At the end of such a vocational program, certificates are awarded for the specific skills acquired.

Many different careers are rooted in a trade school education, such as court reporting, hairdressing, cosmetology—all the way to study for aviation and auto mechanics, plumbers, electricians, carpenters, and sheet metal workers. Trade schools for specific skills such as flying, marine, air navigation and air traffic control also exist, but for that training one is usually directed to the military.

These schools occasionally have particular affiliations with trade unions or industries, or offer certain types of apprenticeship. Although they have not received the best rap in the past, their value and ability to focus on one area of specialization makes them ideal for many students. I once heard a buddy of mine say, "Val is in Court Reporting School and all she really can do is type fast; she has no future." Well, the joke was on him… little did he know, since graduation Val has excelled to the point where she is pulling 75K in Court Reporting!

4. *Work force*
Going directly into the work force after high school is a must for some, but for those trying to escape OLK, this move may very well place you in the top one percent of its members. Generally, those lacking college degrees will earn about half as much as those with them, and such people often struggle to find good jobs that pay well enough to support families, or that even offer health benefits. Though it is perfectly plausible to attend college after several years of working, proving oneself without a college degree until that time is especially difficult. Depending on the type of job being sought, getting interviews becomes a hassle, and promotion of talent and skill during such interviews proves to be even more complicated. Let's face it, a person without a college education is considered a third-tier hire.

Case in point, I know an owner of a business in central Texas. He refuses to hire anyone without a college degree unless the potential employee wants to work on the factory line making minimum wage, which is barely enough to afford an apartment and food. Another friend of mine urged his wife to earn her college diploma before he would marry her, ensuring that she had a plan B in even the most improbable case that something happened to him. What is most important to remember here is the work-force life is not all that it's cracked up to be when you are unable to compete with those who have proven their worth either in college, community college, the military, or trade schools.

5. *Entrepreneur*

A good definition of an entrepreneur is a risk-taker who has the skills and initiative to establish a business. The question posed to anyone in this position involuntarily or who is thinking about the exhilarating world of entrepreneurship is whether he or she has what it takes to be successful ... the right stuff, in other words. Some people do, in spades. Others simply don't have it. If you fall under the latter category, my advice is to go to college, go into the military or trade school, limit yourself to working under another, or develop the qualities that successful entrepreneurs share. Believe it or not, entrepreneurs are not just born. Well, some, of course, seem to be natural-born capitalists, but for the rest of us, such traits can unquestionably be acquired by hard work and application. On this path again, plenty of people along the way are sure to attempt to drag you back into the OLK pack. Nonetheless, if you possess characteristics along the lines of passion, optimism, energy, persistence, and self-responsibility, you can take charge and be your own boss!

David, for instance, never considered it necessary to attend college; He had a successful landscaping business in high school and made more money than most of his friends' parents. Still, after many years he realized it was not all about money and returned to school for a degree in landscape engineering that later added even more credibility to his already-successful business.

As we have seen, there are numerous ways for one to fall into the trap of the OLK and EBB system. Therefore, seek to understand the motivations of those around you in order to make high-quality assessments. By focusing on yourself and your future, you will be able to navigate through the educational and economical mine fields.

Just a quick recap:

James, the guy who never bought a book, it turns out had a photographic memory. The problem transpired when he needed to borrow his roommate's text for the final, which was open book. His roommate had pasted cheat sheets in the pages of the book he let James borrow. Of course, since he never opened it to study, James never became aware of them. Needless to say, he flunked the class because he was accused of cheating and was expelled for breaking the college ethic code. No one knows his current whereabouts.

Though he missed an entire first week of school, Brad finally got it together after a stint in community college. He later graduated from law school and now holds a dream job in Hawaii.

Kenny never made it in pro ball. He spent a couple of seasons in Triple A, and then decided to return to school. After an enormous amount of work to catch up, Ken is now a renowned OBGYN.

Charlie came to the conclusion that college was not for him and started his own business, which has been extraordinarily successful! Being the type that is never fully satisfied, he was quick to recognize that credibility is a vital factor for cautious consumers. People like to know that they can trust the quality of services and investments; they want to get what they pay for and do not want to be deceived. For this reason, he is now considering going back to finish his degree, and to this day wishes he would have just stuck it out for a few more years to begin with.

Mike earned a master's degree in psychology, a master's in business administration, and is currently working on his third masters' degree. We like to call him a professional student, but you would have never guessed that after his OLK experience back during his freshman year.

So the lesson to be learned from these guys… **Do not** get caught up in the Buddy System. It will only end up costing you time, money, and education. Quite frankly, as a young person starting out in the big show, you don't have much of any of these to lose!

Chapter Summary:

1. Watch out for people trying to pull you into OLK.

2. Remember that you do not know the motivations of your fellow-students

3. Other options to consider: community college, the military, trade schools, work force entrepreneur.

4. Don't get caught up in the Buddy System.

5

Greek Therapy

How Fraternities, Sororities and Social Clubs
Can Push for Higher Grades

Want to meet friends you can never forget? Want people to listen, enjoy, and repeat even your dullest or most nonsensical stories? Want a place to begin the search for your soul mate, your best man, or your bridesmaids? Want to take part in activities that will show leadership or seem impressive on a résumé? Such happenings, among others, commonly arise from participation in sororities, fraternities, clubs and groups joined in high school and college. Do not for a second think that you couldn't possibly find your fit in one of these, as there is such an extensive assortment to choose from that it would be extremely difficult for anyone not to find something they like. For that matter, even if this did happen to be the case, the problem could be easily solved by starting a new club!

FRATS AND SORORITIES

If you are thinking about a fraternity or a sorority, keep the following in mind as you go Greek:

Sign up for "Rush" ASAP

Rush is a brief period of time when fraternities and sororities are able to meet and evaluate prospective members. Though it may not be immediately evident, to some extent each has its own distinctive personality. You must strive to find the one that feels at home for you, and not worry yourself with how you might be judged. If you believe you could hang out with a certain group for the remainder of your college years, chances are they probably feel the same. Conversely, if a group doesn't seem to be interested in what you have to offer or if you have to pretend to be someone you're not, it is quite likely that this group is not the right match for you anyway, no matter how luxurious their house is or how great their sports teams do. Keep in mind that the brothers or sisters you acquire through this process are meant to become your home away from home. Yes, it sounds cheesy…but it's true, so make sure they are right for you!

Legacies

Should you have a member of your immediate or extended family who is or was Greek, you would be a legacy in that particular frat or sorority. A letter of recommendation from that family member would almost assuredly produce an invitation to join. However, make sure you do not base your decision to join on your being a legacy. What is right for family members might not be the best for you. Those who do fall under legacy status should get recommendations from other prominent people also.

Don't Slack, Résumés Do Count

A key document for the selection process is your résumé. High school GPA is taken into great consideration, and extracurricular activities are of equal importance. Top priority is given to those with numerous leadership positions, such as class officer, team captain or club president. They are always searching to gain members who have attained honors. Certainly, all honors received at the high school honors convocation would qualify. Likewise, show the award of Eagle Scout as well as any scholarships. Service hours connected with your church, or those performed with organizations such as Big Brothers/Big Sisters, nursing homes, or even those required at some preparatory schools, are all beneficial. National honors such as Academic All-American also are significant. List all volunteer work wherever it may have occurred —even Mission trips—and be sure to include any leadership positions.

Carefully Consider Each Option

During rush, each fraternity and sorority will hold get-acquainted parties, or mixers, after which blanket invitations are issued to those who make their first cut. Each successive party by a fraternity or sorority narrows the field until finally the invitations to join are issued. This process differs slightly between sororities and fraternities, and even among different campuses.

At any rate, when it comes down to having to make a choice between the ones that offered you an invitation, reflect on each extremely carefully before coming to your final decision. Try to picture your future in each one and go with the one that you see yourself excelling in. If you did not get an invitation to join your favorite, do not quit or give up until you are absolutely certain that those who did accept you for who you are aren't what you were looking for after all.

How Fraternities and Sororities Help

Fraternities and sororities can aid you in maintaining or increasing your GPA. In gigantic classes, such as those that far exceed one hundred students, your brothers or sisters can recommend or tell you to avoid professors based on previous experience. This is especially advantageous if it is your first year or if you are taking a course that isn't quite your easiest subject. If you need help in a particular course, some have required study halls or provide tutors, and others have their own personal libraries.

Should your social life be lagging, Greeks periodically have socials at exciting places, sisterhood or brotherhood events, philanthropy events, mixers, semi-formals, and formal dances. Attend all that you can and plan to enjoy each one. Though some are more entertaining than others, and some paired groups are more lackluster than others, it is important to make the most of them. At the very least you can find out what kind of character you do not want to spend the rest of your life with or determine who really proves to be a trusting and true friend, and those reasons alone are worth the effort.

While each individual draws unique experiences and benefits from being in a frat or sorority, several themes run central to all Greek organizations and counter those who criticize Greek life: academic support, personal development, leadership, social opportunities, philanthropy, and networking programs. Let's look at each of these.

Academic Support

The primary reason to enroll in college is to expand your knowledge and obtain a degree. Fraternities and sororities spend a great deal of time enforcing scholastic principles while providing emotional and financial support through academic scholarships. Each chapter maintains standards of minimum grade point averages to pledge, go active, hold office, and remain in good standing.

Personal Development

Greek organizations provide opportunities for each member to develop leadership, time management, financial, and social skills.

Every member is a leader somehow. Whether you are an officer, chair, or simply a committee member, you will learn valuable skills which will assist your everyday life and future.

Social Opportunities

Frats and sororities offer the ideal social life you've looked forward to in college. Being part of the Greek community will provide you with the companionship of close friends, allow you to gain knowledge from people of different backgrounds and experiences, and create a family away from home. Members form friendships unlike any found in other societies. Within each chapter, a bond unites all members. During the years in which members are active, they participate in various social events such as Homecoming Week, Parents' Weekend, Formals, Greek Week, sessions with speakers, philanthropic fundraisers, barbecues, sporting events, and parties. Such activities are not always mandatory, but for those who enjoy mingling, the diversity, range, and just plain fun of the Greek social life is beyond compare.

Philanthropy

Each fraternity and sorority also provides opportunities to participate in several community service programs during the year, both on and off campus, and provide volunteer service to more than just its own members. One of the many advantages is the opportunity to help others. Each serves its own philanthropy, which runs the gamut from cancer awareness to literacy, educational or homeless programs. A great deal of fundraising is dedicated to one's own charitable cause, but even more marvelous are the events held yearly by each frat and sorority where all the other Greeks participate to raise money for each other's causes! They all help each other to help others.

Networking Programs

Networking with people across the United States and abroad, both during and after college, provides Greek members a powerful tool when it comes to sending out résumés, making friends in new places, or asking for recommendations. An old saying still holds strong today, "It's not *what* you know, it's *who* you know." Connections are the key to success. Best of all, Greek affiliation follows members throughout their lives and provides camaraderie among alumni of all organizations for having had a similar college experience, regardless of the specific chapter joined.

Whatever the motivation to join a fraternity or sorority, here are some important points to remember:

1. Usually, a number of fraternities and sororities are on campus; try to get to know each one before you make a decision.

2. First impressions can be misleading. Look beneath the surface and find a solid foundation for evaluating the group.

3. Do not be influenced by stereotypes. When you join the group, you are not joining a name but a closely knit collection of people. They may become your closest friends in college and long after.

4. Pick a group that reflects your interests and will help you develop to your fullest potential.

CLUBS AND GROUPS

You have done your research on fraternities and sororities and were not too impressed. You may be an individualist, a person who has only one or two close friends at a time. Furthermore, you might not find required attendance and mandatory gatherings appealing. Study halls and tutors may perhaps be unnecessary for you. Not to worry. You will find clubs, groups, convocations, and gatherings of all sorts at high schools and colleges. All you have to do is look! Whatever your hobby, avocation, or interest is, undoubtedly there is a club that you can join; but if none exists, start one. This is the time in your life when other responsibilities are not pressing, so spread your wings and enjoy some exciting experiences while you are still able to!

Chapter Summary:

1. Fraternities, sororities, and other clubs or social groups are vital to one's complete education.

2. Sign up for Rush and explore the possibility of a legacy.

3. Your résumé with GPA, leadership positions, honors, service hours, and scholarships will be major determining factors.

4. Sorority get-acquainted parties and fraternity mixers are chances to see and be seen.

5. Fraternities, sororities, and social clubs can help you maintain a solid GPA and provide academic support.

6. Fraternities and sororities can provide one with leadership training, time management, financial aid and social skills.

7. Fraternities and sororities provide for long-lasting friendships, an unparalleled social life, and opportunities to provide community service, philanthropic endeavors, and networking.

8. Independent clubs and social groups can provide much of the same.

6

To Cut or Not to Cut

Sometimes It Is Better to Go Waterskiing

To cut or not to cut a class. That is the question. It must always be answered by you, though it is all too often influenced by others.

Example:

Three roommates are having lunch in the cafeteria and one says, "Why don't we cut class this afternoon and go waterskiing? My boat is ready to go at the lake, and we could be there in an hour." Another one answers, "It's early in the semester, and nothing important is happening in my class." The third one doesn't even think, but says "Sounds great to me, I'm in." Taken in isolation, who would deny them?

Let's consider a few facts:

You are in college to get an education.

Someone has to pay dearly for that education.

A scholarship may be involved.

Your responsibility is to attend class and complete the other college requirements.

Looking at the situation generally, no one would deny a student cutting one class, even for frivolous reasons such as water-skiing or rock climbing. But what would the answer be if three or four classes have already been cut because of illness? What if the class being cut was the first class of the semester, or one of the last three in the semester? Those questions pose completely different situations.

First Class of the Semester

The first class is when the syllabus will be discussed and fleshed out. What to bring to class and how to format and present homework are also learned during this orientation, as well as whether the course contains an online portion and how to access it. The testing procedures will be outlined, and general questions on the availability of extra credit will be answered. Often, the professor will discuss his or her pet peeves and material biases. Some even jump into the material on the first day! This is when you have the chance to make a friend that could very well be the one to save your grade when you need assistance in the course for whatever reason. Hence, the first class is most crucial to success in the course.

Last Classes of the Semester

The last two or three classes in a semester often contain the review of material tested in the final exam. On occasion, actual test questions are discussed under the guise of examples. Some professors even go so far as to give extra credit to those who show they care enough about their grade and future, are passionate enough about the class, or respectful enough of the prof to actually attend these last classes.

By way of explanation concerning the last few classes of the semester, I would like to relate a true story. It took place at a prominent university in the Greater Southwest. Actual names will not be used to protect the innocent:

Toward the end of the semester, one day John didn't feel like attending class. He would not have to convince anyone else, even his roommate, who was taking the same class. He decided to watch TV and get in a short nap so he would be ready for Friday Happy Hour and head downtown later that night. His roommate opted to attend class, and was pleasantly surprised to find the professor using that class period to review the material they had covered since the last test. Throughout the review, the professor was so impressed with the class's answers to the review questions that he made this announcement at the end of the class: "As a result of your attendance at this class and the answers that were given during the review, each of you will be exempt from taking the final." You can be sure John's roommate rubbed it in on the day before the final. John was pouring over his notes and sweating through the review, while his roommate sat watching TV with a cold drink.

Realistically, some students will cut a class for whatever reason. The excuse might be legitimate—such as serious illness—or less than legitimate—such as too tired or more interested in Xbox or shopping. The student who makes the decision to cut a class should be ready likewise to make it worthwhile.

You can make up for skipping by taking these actions:

Schedule an appointment with the professor or T.A.

Explain that you are there to catch up after having missed the previous class.

Ask about the possibility of a summary version of what was presented, such as a copy of the Power Point presentation.

You might ask about other readings that would help bring you up to speed.

If groveling at the professor's feet is not you, other approaches might be used:

Find out who is the best notetaker in the class.

Approach that person and ask if you can copy his or her notes.

Inquire if anything out of the ordinary was covered.

Sometimes the T. A. can help.

Should you strike out with the best notetaker, try the next in line. Eventually you will succeed.

Cutting a class is not the worst thing you could do, and it may well be a great deal of fun and very much worth making it up. After all, it could even produce a story you could tell your children.

On occasion, you will be able to anticipate the need to cut a class. For instance, let us suppose that you plan to travel home (out of state) over the Thanksgiving holiday. Your ride is leaving on the day you have a class. What to do?

Meet with your professor two weeks in advance.

Explain what the situation is.

Ask for advice.

Determine if you can prepare for the missed class, make it up, or scrap the whole idea.

You could be doing so well in the course that the professor says, "Missing that class won't affect your grade." Conversely, he or she might say, "Well now, you are really straddling the line between pass and fail; I would suggest that you not miss the class." If you have done your homework, as outlined in Chapter 3, and have an otherwise acceptable attendance record, the professor should do everything he or she can to be of assistance. At that point, the decision is yours. But, for all practical purposes, it has already been made.

Chapter summary:

1. Cutting a class happens without much thought.

2. Avoid cutting the first class or the last three classes before finals.

3. When you cut a class, make it up.

4. When you anticipate having to cut a class, visit with the professor.

Part Two:
BEATING THE SYSTEM

Part Two Introduction
Beating the System

Rhodes Scholar Techniques that Won't Cost You a Cent

he system visualized in this part of the book is composed of two sets of people. One group is comprised of the professors and their attendant personnel, such as: teaching assistants (TA's), graders (G), administrative personnel, and university hierarchy. The other faction contains the student body. Both parties strive to reach the same definitive goal, though admittedly to varying degrees. That goal is the development and transfer of knowledge to the utmost extent possible. The learning process was once described as the transfer of the teacher's notes to the student's notes without going through the head of either. Though said jokingly, this statement easily becomes a true one when the ultimate goal is, forgotten, however briefly.

In broad terms, most teachers, professors and students want that educational process to be as amiable as possible. Reality proposes that it is the student who must obtain and embrace the active support of the teacher or professor in that transfer procedure. The next few pages address how goal-setting and carefully defined planning aid in elevating grades. Included are lessons concerning how to study teachers and professors, and how to become acquainted with them inside and outside of the classroom. The upcoming information will enable you to recognize how one's resolution to *like* someone psychologically permits him or her to gain more knowledge from that person, and how one's behavior makes efforts successful. Subsequently, you will learn how to ferret out appropriate information with the intention of making intelligent choices, including a section on how electives are possible answers to improving one's GPA and to structuring a career.

7

Cum Laude or Cum Lousy

Higher Grades through Goal-Setting and Preparation

All experienced distance rifle shooters would recommend that one should, "Aim high because the bullet will drop and likely be right on target."

You are in school to learn the material that will form the foundation for further learning, and ultimately a career, correct? Well, it should come as no surprise that the primary way for others to assess your progress and ability is by evaluation of your knowledge and behavior. Given that conduct usually takes an extended amount of time to provide answers, most assessors rely on grades and personal experience. The problem with this stems from the fact that all grades will be on your record, no matter how superb or dreadful. To eliminate the worst from occurring at all, it is best to formulate a plan. A basic starting point is to set your sights on earning an A+ in each class.

**Secret No. 3
Idea
Mapping for
Memorization**

Elements of this grand plan ought to include the course, the teacher or professor, and the behavior you display inside and outside of the classroom. On occasion, a high school or college may dictate what courses are required.

Example:

All freshmen will take English 101. By the same token, only one teacher or professor may be teaching the course. At other times, after declaring a major, you will have to take certain core courses. Fortunately, every curriculum also entails that one must attain a certain number of elective credits, which will be specifically explored in a later chapter.

TIME TO SCHEME

Do Your Research

Before signing up for a course, make an effort to find out as much as possible about the professor who will teach the course. Your student counselor would be a good place to start. There are also websites, such as Rateyourprofessor.com, where students evaluate the prof's personality, the course load, and grading. Fraternities, sororities, and many other special interest clubs or groups might be able to provide information on some of the professors and classes. If all else fails, attempt to meet the professor before signing up for the class. As a last resort, you can drop and add courses to your schedule during the allotted time early in each semester.

Decide Your Fate:

Once you have decided to stick with a class and go all the way, also decide right then and there to end it with an A+ as your final grade.

Design Your Dream Outcome

Obtain the necessary materials: textbooks, notebooks, and other supplies. Sit in the front of the class, at one side or the other, put your eyes on the teacher or professor, and do NOT take them off of them, except to jot a note. (Yes, this also means keep your ears attuned to everything he or she dictates to the class.) We have talked about studying the teacher or professor extensively in Chapter 3. It is a great study technique and just an all-around valuable idea to recopy your notes legibly after the class, even if you are using a laptop.

Prepare Yourself

You must be totally prepared for each class. Assuming that you have already acquired textbooks or similar study materials, also dredge up a highlighter and keep it "attached to your hip," or I guess I should say "your hand." Read the assigned chapters, and if you happen to get caught up in "life" and must be reduced to cramming, at the very least get in the habit of skimming over the text. When you come across something significant, you know what to do! When you have completed a chapter, go back to the highlighted areas and construct an outline or idea map. Keep in mind as you read a chapter that the material will often be in linear form because the author usually accomplishes that feat after the fact. Even at that, most authors will "bird walk"—writer slang for mentioning important information needing to be clarified that is, on occasion, slightly out of line with what is being presented. Although it is possible to compress this information into the linear summary, an idea map would prove to be a more efficient approach, as described next.

Just Plain Brain

Allow me to digress for a moment so that I may present a brief study of the human brain. The brain has two distinct hemispheres separated by a longitudinal fissure and connected by the corpus callosum. In English, the brain is made of two parts that have a gap in between them, and they communicate with one another by sending data over the bridge. Although the hemispheres are quite similar, they tend to differ significantly in their functions. At this juncture we must state emphatically that the words *tend to* are used because the brain is so complex. In certain instances, such as brain injury, split-brained people, or right verses left-handedness, the brain will compensate by having the opposite hemisphere provide the necessary functions.

Keeping this in mind, certain functions are primarily found in either the right brain or the left brain:

Left-brain functions	Right-brain functions
Sequential and orderly	Holistic
Detail-oriented	Uses feeling and emotions
Logical	Imaginative and abstract
Analytical	Intuitive and visual
Verbal (using words and language)	Symbols and images
Present and past	Present and future
Math and science	Philosophy and religion
Knowing	Believing
Pattern	Spatial
Practical	Impetuous
Risk aversion	Risk-taking

A large number of people in any given group is more likely to be left-brain dominant. For that reason, idea mapping is important because it presents a process that encourages right brain or whole brain activity. Not only does it promote a more complete use of abilities but the process also allows for the creative use of simple drawings, as well as various colors that add supplementary imprints on the brain and facilitate memorization. When "Crunch Time" comes around, those students who have used idea mapping are sure to find it much easier to review and memorize seemingly impossible amounts of information.

Time for A Drawing Lesson

To develop an idea map, start with an oval in the center of the paper and list inside it the key concept or target purpose. Next, draw lines radiating from the center oval to new ovals. These are where the major thoughts that support the main idea go. Lines extended from the major lines represent minor supporting details corresponding to the major point of that oval. Shorter lines jut out from the minor branches and represent twigs or attendant material sustaining the minor thoughts. Are you a visual learner? Check out the example on the following page.

Applying idea mapping to this chapter would go as follows. (An illustration is shown below.)

The main idea, topic, or purpose of the chapter is shown in the oval at the center of the paper. In our example:

Higher Grades by Planning, Goal-Setting and Idea Mapping

Major supporting ideas are listed in the ovals at the end of the lines. In our example:

Aim for A+, Idea map, Analyze test results, Learn about prof/course.

Minor pieces of information supporting a major idea would be written on the lighter lines. In our example:

Type all work, Get all materials, Have a plan, Talk with the prof, Use groups, Meet with prof.

Lesser bits supporting the minor thoughts would be shown as twigs. In our example:

Do extra work, and Grades are important.

When working with your linear outline, leave a blank page opposite the one you use for the outline. (In most instances, an idea map will not require a separate page for additions). Have that outline in front of you as the professor presents his or her lecture. Make appropriate notes on the blank page, or add branches to your idea map for clever additions the professor provides during class. This approach will produce a more complete set of notes, since you will have written the bulk of the material beforehand.

IDEA MAP SAMPLE

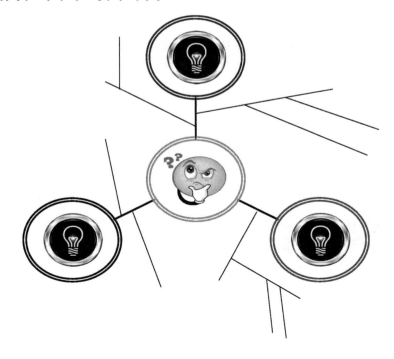

IDEA MAP : THIS BOOK CHAPTER

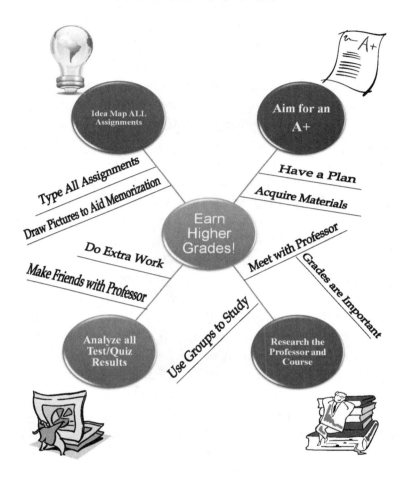

Now Back to Designing Your Dream Outcome

Plan and do the assignments for each class. Type all materials that have to be turned in. Not having to decipher hen-scratching should give you some consideration in the grading process. If assignments are returned, remember to analyze the results whatever your grade may be. If you performed well, try to determine what contributed most to the grade so that process may be subsequently repeated. If you performed poorly, definitely find out what went wrong. Should nothing make sense, schedule an appointment with the professor to remedy the situation. When approached with sincerity, most professors are willing to help. You may even get a chance to do it over, and still get a final grade of an A. In the instance when a do-over does not make sense, you could inquire about creating some other piece of work that would salvage your final grade. Hey, it never hurts to ask!

Behavior outside the classroom is equally important, but more difficult to accomplish because schedules are involved, and those are generally better served when two or three students meet with the professor at the same time. As a case in point, one of the professors I wished to study was in the habit of going over to a small cafeteria in the next building at ten o'clock each morning for coffee. Since students rarely have much discretionary money, the announcement that I was buying coffee always produced a couple of fellow-students who would accompany me to the cafeteria, our ulterior motive being the chance to visit with the professor. Though it didn't happen that often, it was enough to form a relationship with the professor. The resulting interrelationship paid off handsomely for each one of us at the end of the semester! The guiding light is simply this: The more you and other students get to know the professor, the better the professor will perform his duties. Likewise, the students will be more apt to learn and retain. Even in the extreme case when you and the professor are not on the same wave length, being part of a small group with allies who are on board with the professor will provide an opportunity for the beneficial effects to rub off on you.

Remember, grades are imperative and well worth the effort you have to exert to obtain them.

Chapter Summary

1. Aim for an A+ in each class you take. Grades count!

2. Learn all about the professor and the course.

3. Prepare for each class by outlining assigned material and participating.

4. Review your test results and find out where and how you went wrong.

5. Get to know the professor, inside and outside of class.

8

Boost Your GPA...and Your Sanity Level

Basket-Weaving underwater and Other Such Courses

"If I am assigned one more task, I am going to go insane!" You know this phrase, and you know it well. We've all had such moments where it seems we have too much on our plates and no room left to stomach it all! As a student, chances are slim to none that this pressured feeling will not come about at one point or another. So if it has not happened to you yet, prepare yourself.

No matter what the major, required course loads often seem relentless at first glance. Fortunately, the wise idea came about some time ago that students should obtain an eclectic education as a foundation and aid to their major focus. After this monumental proposal took flight, it became essential for one not solely to learn the "tricks of their trade," so to speak, but to become cultured in various subjects such as foreign language and the arts, as well. Hence, electives were born. Ironically, the supplementary course work actually proved to ease such feelings of overexertion and to assist in improved grade point averages!

Today, high schools and colleges around the world require students to complete a certain number of elective credit hours (or fresh-air courses) before graduation. Before deeming such classes a joke, or a pointless waste of time and brain space, take what is said here into consideration. You will soon find—if you have not done so already—that electives are wonderful opportunities to experience and obtain knowledge in areas that spark your interest or curiosity; areas that might not coincide with your career choice in the slightest! More important, taking part in classes that you enjoy tends to result in grades that will boost your GPA. A word of caution, however: , Even your closest friends may perhaps stab you in the back if you do not choose such courses wisely!

Elective: The Best Friend

Let's talk about the first outcome, because that is the most likely and the easiest to consider. In basic terms, an elective is a course you decide to take that is likely outside of your major or minor. The elective therefore should be subject matter that excites you. With a positive attitude exuding from that excitement, half the battle is won. You are prone to be all ears on the first day of class, as you well should be. Listen exclusively as the professor describes what will be covered, when tests will occur, if a paper will be required, and so forth. Since you are eager to learn, the whole process most frequently will flow smoothly. Make sure you excel in each part, thereby taking advantage of the chance to receive a higher grade and raise your GPA.

In other instances, the decision will not be so automatic. The goal is to select a course you expect to enjoy that will allow you some relaxation while still resulting in a fine grade. This is where ingenuity comes in. To begin with, avoid all pass/fail courses, as they waste the opportunity to enhance your GPA.

If you are athletically inclined, you might consider a physical education course that will enable you to have fun as you get an A. If you happen to be a history or film buff, some of those courses might just be what you need.

When all else fails, turn to your relationships for information. If you are a member of a fraternity, talk to the brothers. As a sorority member, some sisters assuredly would be willing and able to provide some input as to which classes to mull over. Likewise, there are dozens of clubs, groups, and organizations you are possibly involved in. Discuss your options with your companions to discover what courses and professors provide a less challenging experience and a high probability of an A.

Elective: The Backstabber

Even with all that advice, the situation is fraught with danger, as a university student and longtime friend of mine has so described: He had selected what he thought was the perfect elective course. At the all-important first class, he discovered that the professor's requirements for an A would take more time and effort than attending two courses. He dropped it immediately. Procrastination put him in a time bind, so he sought advice from an upperclassman. His would-be advisor admitted that he didn't know much about it, but that he had taken such and such course and breezed through it with an A. My friend signed up for the course only to discover that the upperclassman was a genius and breezed through *all* his classes with an A—another dropped course and a lost opportunity.

With that input, you will have to take your chances. Be at class on that powerful first day when the syllabus is detailed and discussed. Ask every question you can think of to help you determine what kind of classroom experience this course will provide. If you are still in doubt, make an appointment with the professor during office hours. That visit will allow for questions that might be too delicate for the class-at-large. Talk about the planned tests and any possible prerequisites that could preclude your earning a higher grade. It is far better to find out early that you might be selecting a course that will jeopardize your GPA rather than help it. At that point, you will still have time to use the drop/add process without penalty.

Subsequently, you will be free to try again. Unfortunately, this attempt will not be as simple. You can select another course, but you will likely miss the first class of your second choice. You will then have to visit at length with the professor or the TA to search out all the information you will need to make a "go–no-go" decision on that second choice, or live with whatever happens.

Look upon electives as a possible back door to Planning. As a young undergraduate, I entered the university in the field of engineering. When given the chance to choose electives, I was most excited about psychology and took psychology courses at every opportunity. During my junior year, I became disenchanted with engineering work and began thinking about switching majors. The decision was simple when I thought, *Why not make my avocation my new vocation?* Fortunately, I had all the prerequisite courses completed, and the change to a psychology major was enacted seamlessly. In that case, electives played an extremely important role in my ultimate career choice.

The whole idea is to make the best use of the opportunities that electives provide, while avoiding unseen and unpleasant surprises. In the final analysis, do as complete a job as possible in all your classes. Some will be less challenging than others. Attempt to get an A in all of your courses and make the job as easy as you possibly can.

So what is the secret to remaining sane while maintaining high educational standing in the midst of continuous and complicated chaos? Electives!

Chapter Summary:

1. Electives can be an invitation to increase your grade point average.

2. Acquire appropriate information about professors and courses.

3. Courses you like will generally be easiest for you.

4. Choose wisely so as not to jeopardize your grade point average.

PART THREE

The Right Way to Study for Exams

Part Three Introduction
The Right Way to Study for Exams

The Simple Way to Save Time and Accumulate Grade Points

Time to study up on how to study! Yes, you read that correctly: In this part of the book, we will talk specifically about how to prepare for exams and how to study for and take various types of tests. By now, you have probably construed that you must study continuously the whole year through in order to produce high-quality results. Studying is done throughout the semester and in a more determined way at test time. The entire process relies on the outlining or idea mapping done before, during, and after classes.

Attendant material will be presented on where to study and how to study, as well as where *not* to study. The pros and cons of group study halls are examined along with the benefits of a study plan.

Test-taking advice is divided into: true-false, multiple choice, fill in the blanks, matching and essay. Particular attention is given to preparation for each type of test. Specific tips for creative versions of test items and caveats against typical student mistakes such as the first-instinct fallacy will be discussed.

Finally, you will find valuable information on the memorization process so necessary for exam time. Convincing evidence will be provided for cramming the night before tests to ensure that the trigger outline or idea map will provide the facts necessary for a grade that will increase your grade point average.

9

Sitting Down to Business

Where Not to Study and Why

Everyone has a preferred way to study. Naturally, the way that works for you is the best way. The major concern in this chapter is where not to attempt it. Much depends on where and how you studied in high school because that setting will likely be most comfortable for you. Of course, at that time, limited options prevailed. You may have had a study hall period which made the decision easy. The other major option was in your room at home. Likewise, you may have had music playing softly in the background as you poured over the books and worked on assignments.

Old Habits Live Easy

College will present additional options and complications. Generally, you should strive to create the same conditions each time you study. If you were previously accustomed to semi-quiet surroundings with soft background music, you should try to provide that basic setting. On the other hand, you may have been addicted to having the TV or radio on in the room. So be it.

Comfortable Confusion

Never study while in bed. However tempting that may be, avoid it at all costs. You confuse your body with two diverse tasks: sleeping vs. purposeful studying. Making the critical mistake of conditioning yourself to associate study time with sleeping produces unwanted results. Consequently, the mind might generalize such a sleeping response to the classroom and produce a colossal problem. Some students, however, are accustomed to sprawling out on the floor while tackling assignments. A tip for those who must study this way: Periodically shake yourself, stand up, or sit up straight momentarily to remind your body to remain alert and active.

Oh, Give Me a Break

Every so often you need to take a change-of -pace break. Do something completely different. Even studying a completely different subject, preferably one you enjoy, will produce the desired effect. If the occasion allows, it would be greatly beneficial for you to engage in some physical activity, such as foosball, a game of ping pong or taking a walk. A half hour of such exercise will prepare you for a more effective study period by increasing your endorphins and attentiveness.

Assuming that you have established for yourself the ideal circumstances for studying, your mission is to discover where you can find or produce such conditions. Your bedroom will be the first candidate. Since most students will have one or more roommates, you may or may not have a problem. If you prefer a noisy atmosphere with music, TV, and conversation, you are right at home and ready to study.

If you need a relatively quiet background, however, you have your work cut out for you. You might be able to come to an agreement with your roommates to establish a study time of a certain amount of hours when background noise is controlled. One enterprising student found that his roommates had no morning classes so they slept late. He used that hiatus to study.

Second, third, and fourth-year students often band together and move off campus. One critical requirement should be to agree on the study time environment. Setting aside one room just for study purposes often proves rewarding. When it comes to needing a quiet space, the library is perfect, as it provides such accommodations as internet connection, photocopy machines, rare archives, and usually a snack bar or vending machines. However, those who deem reading aloud as a crucial study tactic might have to stay away from this student powerhouse. If you fall into this category, consider possibly studying at a park or in a courtyard outside of classroom buildings or contained within apartment complexes. A backyard would work as well, if your residence happens to be party central! Such spots also provide the benefits of fresh air, and they help one avoid feelings of confinement. It may sound silly, but another recommended spot is inside a car, which also helps if the weather hinders the outdoor locations. Studying in a vehicle allows students to situate themselves in advantageous positions, such as in the parking lot of a basketball court to be utilized during a study break, or outside of a classroom during a final review of study materials. Just remember to keep the A/C on or the windows down!

Desperate Times Call for Desperate Measures

You may find yourself extremely tired just about the time you are to begin studying. I found that for me it was better to set an alarm, go to sleep for a few hours, and wake up refreshed and ready to study.

Food can also provide you with a problem. It is far better to take a snack break, rather than to keep hitting the books, which is simply counter-productive. Equally problematic is eating too much. When you are overly full, you become sluggish and unable to concentrate. So when it comes to study time, plan to eat lightly.

Keep in mind that you can study almost anywhere, provided you shut out all distractions and focus on the task at hand. For instance, if I were memorizing a list of words and had the flash cards available, I could study while standing in line waiting for a snow cone. A quick run-through of the cards was all I needed for one trial. Completing the test trials repeatedly at off times accomplished the task of memorizing far more easily than an hour of concentrated cramming. Other types of study, such as that requiring deep concentration, would call for your ideal study conditions at a place similar to the library, your room, outside, or in a car.

Chapter Summary:

1. Determine your ideal study conditions and duplicate them at study times.

2. Do not study in bed. The results are counterproductive.

3. Have a plan to counter situations such as being too tired or too hungry to study.

4. Be ready to study at off times.

10

Group Study Halls

Misery Loves Company

Group study halls can be anything but study. In some instances, certain groups are required to attend study hall. The three most prominent categories are student athletes, Greeks, and freshmen. The mere fact that it is required may deter many students from regular use.

However, every student should visit a study hall or study group, even if it has not been a requirement to do so. To one's surprise, the experience could be eye-opening in one sense and almost delightful in another! Assume that currently your experience has left you somewhere in the middle and you haven't been completely turned off. As an aside, it is highly likely that being required to attend has jaundiced you from that point on. However, for these purposes you will remain neutral.. You have just finished a class. You have forty-five minutes to burn and the study hall is en route to your next class.

Before you decide to head for the study hall, be sure to have a plan in mind. If you show up merely to see what is happening, you will be contributing to the reason study halls have a poor reputation. Your actions will be random and most likely result in the chaotic surroundings caused by random behavior. Instead, be ready to do something constructive on the spur of the moment. If you have just come from a class, you might clean up your notes and then carefully review what you learned. After all, notes reviewed within seventy-two hours of learning have significantly greater probability of being remembered. Always have material in your backpack that must be read for some class. If you are memorizing something, having the flash cards with you is ideal. You could quickly go through a list of vocabulary words a few times.

Those that have a plan are far more likely to get things done. Think through the day and, in the process, an assignment will often trigger the need to take the appropriate materials with you.

You can seek out a quiet area in the study hall, and go about your planned tasks. As you set the tone of quiet study, often kindred souls who wish to do the same will find you. Generally, others will be far more likely to join you in quiet study than to start in a new direction. You probably will make a couple of new friends! Who knows? Maybe you will find similarities in your class schedules and be able to review each others' notes. I would like to share a story about a study hall experience that might encourage those of you who find them dull and unnecessary to give them another try.

Philosophy class was an interesting, yet grueling, subject for me. I had a test in a couple of hours, so I decided to attend the study hall for some last- minute review. It was here that I met the person that would soon become my study buddy and my best friend. I sat down at a table, and within minutes she came up and asked if I was getting ready to take Trig's Philosophy test. We compared notes, both finding material that wasn't in our own, and sure enough, we both aced that test. As it turned out, we had each been hoping to ask the professor a few questions, so we banded together to study him as well. We noticed that he rode his bicycle to class each day, so one afternoon we staked out at the bike rack and awaited his return. We proceeded to spend the rest of our free period joking around with Professor Trig, as well as taking in some much-needed advice about the final and some particular points to remember about Kierkegaard and fikta for the next test. We were so proud of ourselves for accomplishing so much that we decided to celebrate that night. Needless to say, we passed that class with flying colors, Trig became a wonderful candidate to write a recommendation for me, and that fellow-student and I remain best friends to this day! All of this was due to my going to a single study hall.

Should all turn out to be a lost cause, you always have options. You may join a chat group and make new friends. Get a cup of coffee. Head out to your next destination. As you can tell, it never hurts to try it out!

High school study halls will likewise run the gamut. Some may be the site of punishment, constructive leisure, concentrated study, or general free-for-all discussion. Too often the study hall is an exercise in discipline for the unlucky teacher assigned to that session.

The same study rules should apply in high school. Have a plan for study hall time. With little else to do, and having the benefit of some study hall supervision, you can get your assignments done, thereby avoiding guilt at home when your favorite TV program airs.

One benefit of study hall I should mention is that many of them will provide tutors, often without cost. Do not pass up the chance to get a leg up on some aspect of a subject you find totally confusing. Become familiar with and take advantage of the many resources high schools and colleges provide.

Should you be a member of the special groups required to attend study hall anyway, make it a point to become well-acquainted with a couple of the tutors. When the need arises at any time during college, at least you will already know someone who might aid in your studies. And, when you know someone and have faith in their capabilities, you will learn more from them and at a faster rate!

Chapter summary:

1. Have a study plan when you go to the study hall, especially if required to be there.

2. Be sure you always have with you required reading and material to be memorized.

3. Get to know and take advantage of tutors.

11

Multiple Guess

How to Study for and Take Objective Quizzes

All progress toward a goal is dependent upon feedback. It comes in many forms, such as: pop quizzes, scheduled tests, midterms, review tests, and final exams. These assessments are meant to provide answers to the questions:

What do you know?

To what extent do you know it?

How well can you apply it?

They are also a monitor for the teacher or professor to evaluate his or her own abilities. The single best way for you to get ready for such examinations is the Scouts' motto,

Be Prepared.

By now you have recognized that the whole process starts with preparing for class by outlining or idea mapping

**Secret No. 4
First Instinct
Fallacy**

the assigned material, and taking notes in the classroom. If you have diligently re-copied or idea mapped the notes after each class, you will find it much easier to become organized for tests.

As we've mentioned elsewhere in the book, becoming a student of your professor is essential to success. Spend some time during regular office hours talking with the professor about his or her testing approach.

There are five major types of tests:

1. True-False

2. Multiple-Choice

3. Fill in the Blanks

4. Matching

5. Essay

Find out which one or ones will be utilized in each class. Try to obtain sample questions, which often will provide a feel for the degree of difficulty. Be sure to ask the professor if guessing will be penalized. Occasionally, professors score a test by taking the number of correct test answers and subtracting the number of incorrect answers, or some percentage of the number incorrect, with the final score being the result of those two numbers. Test items left blank in this case are not counted as missed. Generally this penalty is applicable only to true/false tests. Though this does not happen often, you will find that it does happen. When it does, you will benefit greatly from knowing!

Given the aforementioned information, you will be able to study the material using the testing format that the teacher or professor prefers.

Example:

If true/false is the preferred approach, study the material in statement form. The statements will be either true or false. A preference for multiple-choice questions requires studying the material in the form of lists. Although the study process was covered in an earlier chapter, suffice it to say you should study by yourself first, and if time permits repeat the session in a small group.

As discussed before, always use the distributed times in study; that is, study for an allotted time and then do something else such as reading or studying a different subject. Return for another period on the original subject until your study time is up. In high school, an intriguing teacher of mine for a Communications class mentioned this in a lecture:

Due to attention span, students generally remember best the first fifteen and last fifteen minutes of each study session. Therefore, the wise student would study for thirty minutes, break, study for another thirty, break, and so on. That way, he or she will remember the first fifteen and last fifteen minutes, or the total of each session!

Although this has not been thoroughly tested, it makes sense to an extent, and I never forgot it. This technique surely aided in my memory skills when utilized in college!

Instances will arise where the question becomes, "Should I study the whole or only part of the material?" The answer to that question lies in the type of material you are studying. If, for example, you are trying to memorize a speech, go through the whole speech. If you are studying vocabulary words using flashcards, test your recall on part of the list. When successful, continue with the remainder of the list.

Test time

- ✐ Come prepared.
- ✐ Review the directions thoroughly.
- ✐ Circle crucial words, such as: *Not, Always, Never, Sometimes,* etc.

🖋 Determine how much time you can spend on each question.

🖋 Leave time for a quick review to make sure your answer sheet is filled in correctly and that you haven't made any simple mistakes.

As is true for all tests, you must bring the appropriate materials for the test in question. They will include: paper, pencils, pens, erasers, Scantrons or essay booklets; on occasion the textbook, calculator, a bottle of water, if allowed. When you receive the test, begin by putting your name and appropriate information on the paper and then do a brief review. Notice specific instructions. Look for the word *Not* and circle it. Calculate the amount of time that should be allowed for each question or section of the test. Allow for time at the end to review your answers and correct any glaring errors.

Now there is disagreement among test-taking advisors. Some will say you should go through the entire test, answering the easier questions first, while marking those that were not attempted. The rationale is that answering questions will give you confidence and may provide a clue to answering more difficult questions. Others say, "Don't skip around, as you may miss answering important questions because you didn't see that they were un- answered." Be your own judge as to which way will work best for you.

True/False Questions

○ Pay attention to every word

○ Avoid First-Instinct Fallacy.

○ Read through the remainder of test questions and answers in order to trigger information in your mind pertaining to questions that you are unsure of the answer

○ Again, heed special attention to answer-altering words, such as *Not*

When answering True/False questions (see page 203 for test item examples), read the question very carefully, paying attention to every word. Think about the statement thoroughly and then mark it as true or false. At all costs, avoid what is called, "First-Instinct Fallacy" (Kruger, Wirtz, & Miller). Their research (see pages 201-202) indicates that test takers have a deeply ingrained belief they should not change a first-instinct answer when, in fact, most changes are from wrong to right. Instead, you should change your answer when these situations occur. Suppose you have difficulty deciding which answer you should choose. Later in the test, a statement might appear that triggers the answer to an earlier question where you chose the wrong answer. You could suddenly spot the word "not," which changes everything, and you see you selected the wrong answer. New information pops into your head and you now know the correct answer, with no doubt in your mind.

A research article abstract, on the efficacy of changing a test answer titled, "Counterfactual Thinking and the First-Instinct Fallacy," by Kruger, Wirtz, & Miller, as reported in *The Journal of Personality and Social Psychology* Volume 88, pages 725 to 735 © 2005 by the American Psychological Association, reprinted with permission states:

Most people believe that they should avoid changing their answer when taking Multiple-Choice tests. Virtu-ally all research on this topic, however, has suggested that this strategy is ill-founded. Most answer changes are from incorrect to correct and people who change their answers usually improve their test scores. Why do people believe in this strategy if the data so strongly refutes it? The authors argue that the belief is in part a product of counterfactual thinking. Changing an answer when one should have stuck with one's original answer leads to more "if only..." self-recriminations than does sticking with one's first instinct when one should have switched. As a consequence, instances of the former are more memorable than instances of the latter. This differential availability provides individuals with compelling (albeit illusory) personal evidence for the wisdom of always following their first instinct, with suboptimal test scores the result.

You may have heard the infamous saying, "When in doubt, Charlie out," meaning to choose C as your answer if you are unsure on a test question. However, this is not a wise decision, as most teachers have also heard this and arrange their test answers accordingly. It is far better to use the multiple-guess method.

Multiple-Choice Tests

- 📖 Determine which possible answers are definitely incorrect
- 📖 When "none of," or "all of the above" are answer choices, determine if more than one answer makes sense
- 📖 Eliminate two answers and treat the remainder using the true/false process

For multiple-choice tests (see pages, 203-204 for test item illustrations), the usual method of presentation is a stem or partial sentence with a blank space at the end and four or more possible alternative answers. Here again, some test takers advise that you should read the stem and attempt to answer the question without looking at the possible answers. Once you have formulated your answer, read the individual answers to determine which one comes closest to your proposed answer. Should you not be able to decide on an answer or you are not sure, keep in mind that with such multiple-choice items, usually one or two answers are obviously wrong. Find those two and immediately remove them from consideration by striking the attendant letters or numbers. One of the remaining two choices is the correct answer. Treat each of the remaining two answers as a true/ false item. Carefully read the stem along with one of the remaining two choices and say to yourself, "True or false?" Note your immediate response. Read the stem along with the remaining alternative. Treat it like a true/ false statement. Think about it and again note whether you feel the last selection was true or false. At that point, you should be able to arrive at a reasonable decision.

Special situations

On occasion, multiple-choice test items may include the response, "all of the above" or "none of the above." If you know definitely that two or three possible answers are correct, seriously consider the answer to be "all of the above." The choice "none of the above" is far rarer in tests, but if it occurs use the above procedure as described in the answer "all of the above" as your decision methodology.

When multiple-choice test items contain numbers, the convention is to eliminate the highest and lowest answers and choose among the remaining ones. Even in the face of that advice, I have always attempted to solve the number problem in approximate terms, to determine if the answer approximated the highest or lowest solution. That information helped to justify eliminating the highest and lowest alternatives. In a recent national publication, The National Psychologist, that provided continuing education credit for answering questions developed from articles, two math questions conformed to dropping the highest and lowest answers.

Having worked with test development, I discovered that it generally requires more words to state the correct answer and fewer words to develop incorrect ones. So, look more carefully at longer alternatives. If you do not have a clue as to what is correct, and there is no penalty for guessing, choose the longest one. Keep in mind that any stem that is grammatically incorrect with an answer is a sure giveaway that the selected answer is incorrect. Likewise, beware of choices that incorporate generalized words such as *all, every, always, never,* and *none.* Such words usually invalidate the answer.

Fill in the blank

❖ Look at the size of the blanks, and the number of blanks

❖ Pay attention to conjugation and grammar for a dead giveaway

Fill-in-the-blank test items are not often used in higher education classes. Since such items *do* occur in tests given to smaller-size classes, such as within one's major, or at smaller schools, we will briefly discuss them (see page 205 for test item illustrations). This type of test item requires one to be more of a detective. First, look at the size of the blank. A short length indicates a single word. A longer blank probably means two or more words. The context of the question is likely to indicate whether you are looking for a name, a date, or some isolated piece of information. As mentioned in the section on multiple-choice questions, the grammar should tip you off to what the fill-in answer is. Fill-in-the-blank items also provide you with the opportunity to demonstrate correct spelling and the use of proper grammar. In your response to such items, be sure that you do not provide information outside the scope of the question. The best advice for fill-in-the-blank type tests is to be even better prepared with the material being tested.

Matching

> ➤ Determine beforehand what material will be on the tests; whether dates or full names will need to be recalled.

> ➤ Make a timeline in your notes to facilitate study should the need arise.

> ➤ Verify what time period each test will cover in order to eliminate supplemental choices.

Matching as a test item has been gaining in popularity (see pages 205-206 for test item illustrations). An item consists of two columns: The first column entries are often numbered; the second column entries use the alphabet. The object is to match a numbered item with a lettered item indicating that the two entries matched are related in the correct sense. Preparation for a matching test requires you to study the various concepts thoroughly so as to know their connectability. For instance, when studying history, events are often related to the date of their occurrence. Hence, the matching test item would present a column of dates and a column of events. The requirement would be to match an event with its correct date of occurrence. Occasionally, the matching test item will have more entries in one column than there are in the other column. Example:

There could be more dates than events. This method eliminates a forced answer to the last pairing.

Recall our discussion about studying the teacher or professor; it is imperative that you determine if the matching test items will be used. In the event that the answer is yes, try to determine what relationship will be used.

Example:

Event/date, literary work/author, event/country, game/equipment, championship/team. Study with those possibilities in mind.

By utilizing these tips during study and while taking tests, you will be more focused and find it easier to deduce the correct and incorrect answers to test questions.

Chapter Summary

1. Learn to take appropriate notes.

2. Find out what types of questions will be used and study accordingly.

3. True/False items call for first impressions, but should be changed when deemed most probably incorrect after thorough consideration.

4. Multiple Choice: eliminate two alternatives; treat the remaining alternatives as true/false items.

5. Fill in the Blank: the blank size and wording may be clues.

6. Matching test items will require the study of relationships.

12

The Beast from 20,000 Footnotes

The Essay Exam and How to Ace It

When you put your pencil or ballpoint pen to a notebook or blue book, you are doing more than demonstrating how much you know about a subject. What you are really doing is participating in a contest, a game of skill, in which everyone in the class participates.

To the winners, a nice array of prizes will be awarded. The top ten percent or so get the first-place awards (A's); figure twenty percent for the second-place winners (B's); also-rans, roughly forty percent are stuck with the C trophies; finally, the bottom thirty percent come away with the booby prizes. Accumulate too many "boobies" and you don't get to participate in any more contests.

Grades, then, are relative. An A in one government class may only be worth a C in another, depending on how well the class does as a whole. In a typical "curve," the highest grade

Secret No. 4
continued
Test
Preparation

gets the A; the lowest an F. The others are distributed in between on the 10-20-40-20-10 formula illustrated above.

Naturally, if you can get in a class full of morons, your chances of scoring the A are sizably increased, and you won't have to work so hard for it, since the object of the game is not to answer all the questions, but to accumulate more points than anyone else. The higher up the point scale, the better your chance of being king of the mountain.

The favorite implement of torture at exam time is the essay examination. But why the essay, we ask? Whatever happened to good old multiple guess or true-false? "Sorry about that," reasons the prof, but the essay is the only true method of measuring how much you know.

Well, that's the way he sees it. Actually, essay exams rarely call for any deeper exercise in logical thinking or critical analysis. What's really asked for is a regurgitation of facts.

When called upon to compare and contrast (a favorite essay gambit) the foreign policies of Sweden and Denmark, what it really means is, describe the foreign policy of Sweden and the foreign policy of Denmark, with a few phrases tossed in here and there ("Sweden, on the other hand," "Similarly, Denmark...") just to show you haven't forgotten how the question was phrased. If you can amass more facts than your neighbors, you'll get a higher grade. Just make sure to answer the actual question at hand.

Don't be misled by the foregoing paragraph. Do read the essay question thoroughly to interpret exactly what is asked. Although you will generally be weaving facts into your answer, the request for an explanation is likely to require giving reasons for, or the causes of, an outcome. To nail down an A you will often have to show the logical developments or the resulting relation-ships brought about by the process. To interpret will require you also to explain the meaning of the facts you are relating. Being able to recall the facts most likely will trigger the causes, reasons, developments, and explanations, because these provide the glue that holds those facts together.

Taking an essay exam is like wandering into an open field full of gold nuggets. For the allotted test time period, you may meander about the field to your heart's content, gathering as many nuggets as you may chance to find. At the end of the time cycle, everyone cashes in his or her treasure, and whosoever shall cash in the greatest number of nuggets gets a golden crown, and shall live happily ever after (until the next test, of course)!

The trick is to collect all the nuggets, "all" meaning more than anyone else, before the time runs out. Not an easy task, considering the great wealth of goodies hidden about. Some will be rather obvious, of course, sitting bright and beautiful on the surface. But everyone's going to lay claim to these obvious baubles, so their value is second-rate. To really strike it rich, we must get at the hidden treasure underneath the rich mother lode, not quite so obvious on first reading.

How do we collect all the "fool's gold," and reach the hard-to-get-at nuggets of real gold beneath the surface as well? The key is to plot the location of the goodies before the exam actually begins, carefully cataloging each precious fact where it may be immediately retrieved.

There is one and only one way in which this ambitious feat may be accomplished, and that oh-so-important method is the subject of this chapter.

Step 1: underlining/highlighting

Underlining or highlighting is the same for both essay and objective type exams. Let's assume you've already completed this step described in Chapter 7 and you are ready for Step 2.

Step 2: The Master Outline

Highlighter or ballpoint ready? Turn back to the beginning of the chapter, take a deep breath, and begin ….outlining/idea mapping.

At this point you're probably cowering under the library table or heaving this book into the biology pond. Why students have such a horror of outlining/idea mapping, I'll never understand. I might just as well have advised translating the assignment into Hittite. They flee from it like the Medusa's head—the scourge of the studying class, which must be avoided at any cost—and more often than not, the cost is a drop in grade.

This widespread revulsion is the very reason why you should rush to embrace the outlining/idea mapping method. It is the only true and accurate system for nailing down and cataloging all those lovely nuggets before the exam starts. The others are all hit-or-miss.

So let the others read their notes, re- read the textbook, do outside reading, and any other method they so choose. They'll never get to Jericho without a map, and that's what the outline/idea mapping is: a carefully worked out ground plan to success.

When to Outline/Idea Map

The best time to outline or idea map is immediately after you've done your highlighting or underlining. This way, the filler material cementing those facts together is fresh in your mind and its correlation will be carried over to your outline or idea map. Also, when you have a fresh and clear picture of the entire chapter content, the logical outline pattern comes easily and naturally.

How to Outline/Idea Map

It isn't necessary to follow the traditional outlining pattern taught back in elementary school:

I.
  A.
    1.
      a.

Of course, if that system works best for you, fine. I personally prefer to drop the A's and B's entirely. The reason is that there are so many times you are called upon to list certain facts or events and I always found it easier to recall there were seven reasons why Albert Schweitzer never got snake bitten, rather than having to count A-B-C-D-E-F-G. Consequently, my outline looks like:

I.
  1.
    <u>1</u>.
      (1)

For the full process of idea mapping, refer to Chapter 7. In summary, you start the idea map with an oval in the center of a piece of paper. Write the chapter title in that oval. Draw lines radiating from the center oval to the outside placing an oval at the end. Major ideas are written in the ovals. Draw lines jutting out from the major ideas like branches on a tree. Supporting minor points would be placed on the branches. See illustration on the next page.

The important thing is that you boil off all the water, so that your outline or map becomes a simple, concise stock containing all the juicy, succulent facts of which A papers are made.

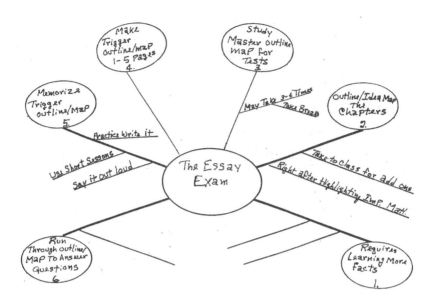

Neatness and organization are doubly important, even though no one will see the outline or map but you. Weeks, even months later, when you return for that final ordeal, you don't want to feel like Napoleon trying to decipher the Rosetta Stone. If your handwriting looks like it was scrawled by an arthritic chimpanzee that has had too much to drink, your miseries at exam time will be two-fold. You can avoid this unnecessary exasperation by typing your master outline or redrawing your map when you have completed the work. If you don't type (you should learn), take the extra time to write neatly and in well-defined block form.

Finally, outline or map on the front side of the page only, leaving the next page blank. Keep the pages in a loose-leaf notebook (one for each course), and it's a good idea to take to class only those pages you'll be discussing that day. Misery is losing all your study notes three-quarters of the way through the semester.

Step 3: Throw Away Your Textbook

After you've completed your master outline or idea map, you are finished with that section of the text. Do with it what you like: file it away, hock it, burn it on the steps of the administration building (just kidding). All you'll need now is that precious little outline or map, for if you've done your job correctly, it's as good as your textbook—minus about three-fourths of a ton of filler material.

Step 4: In the Classroom

Drag your prepared outline or idea map to class with you and keep it smack dab in front of your eyeballs throughout the semester. Follow it and you should be able to respond to most any question or point of discussion that arises. Even if you're daydreaming or half asleep, when a surprise question hits you from out of the blue, a quick glance at your printed outline should bring your thoughts quickly into focus.

Don't be afraid to make marks on it either. If the professor seems to dwell at length on one particular topic, so note in your outline or map. If observations are made in class that did not appear in the text, note them on the blank page directly opposite the pertinent section of your prepared notes, or draw another branch on your idea map.

You will be amazed at the time and frustration this method will save! No longer must you be frantically scribbling out facts and figures, breathlessly grabbing for the pearls as they are cast from the lectern. Most of those factual gems will already be safely stored away on your outline or map, and those few that aren't, may be easily added on the opposite blank page. Now you can relax, concentrate on the lecture, participate in the discussion, (your outline will be of great help in demonstrating to the professor how intelligent you are), or just gaze out the window, dreaming about greater things to come—such as Friday night's social.

Step 5: The Quickie Outline/Map

1. *First Run-Through*

A few nights before the big test, take steps to prepare the "Quickie Outline/Map." First, sit down and carefully read through the master outline or map along with any classroom notations, from start to finish.

On first reading, this may take some time. Remember: This is heavy stuff—an entire unit or course concentrated into twenty or thirty typewritten pages or idea maps. It may take you an hour or more just to read through it with understanding. If any part of it seems hazy, go back to the text and read the underlined or highlighted portions in order to refresh your memory. You may wish to draw stick figures or other pictures on your map to help you remember. Just be sure that when you finish that first reading, you have touched upon and understand everything covered in the course. At this point, it is not necessary that you be able to recall all that information. We'll come back to that in a few minutes.

2. *Subsequent Run-Through*

Now (after a brief break), go back and read the material through a second time. It will be easier reading this trip, and you should finish it in at least half the time it took you before. At this point you should begin feeling more confident about the material. Nevertheless, resist the urge to split for the TV lounge.

Reread the outline or map again and again and again until you are so thoroughly familiar with the material that when you read it, you have no sense of interest there whatsoever. It becomes difficult to concentrate; the material has become so second nature. In fact, your mind will be more or less running ahead of your eyes as you read.

This is around the time when you must really fight to resist the siren's call beckoning to you from television land. Even though you feel like you know that material backwards and forwards, unless you can reproduce it—the outline/map—from memory, you're still not fully prepared. For the difference between an A and a B, read on....

3. *Making the Trigger Outline/Map*

Now—and only now—after you are thoroughly familiar with all the material, go back and re-outline or idea map! Boil the material down to the bare bones—one- two- five pages or less.

This outline or map will be different than your master outline in that it will be incomplete at first. It may contain only the major divisions of the master, along with a few pictures and subsequent headings or branches to spur your imagination in difficult areas. Remember: The trigger outline/map is not a detailed analysis of the course. It is a checklist whereby the more complex details of the larger notes may be instantly and systematically called to mind.

The trigger outline or map may contain only keywords, a picture, a catch phrase perhaps, or even nonsense jargon to trigger your thinking. You might incorporate picture diagrams; include anything, so long as it triggers your mind to recall what is detailed in the master outline. Once you have sketched out this final memory tool, move on to the final step—Memorization.

Step 6: Memorization

Hopefully, the trigger outline or map will be short enough that it may be committed to memory inside of thirty minutes or an hour. You may be surprised to find you can reproduce it on the second or third try. For longer "triggers" (and I've memorized some year-long courses numbering ten hand- written pages), here are some tips for faster memorization:

> *Start with a handwritten sloppy trigger outline or map.* No need for neatness or typewritten work here. You'll find that your mind will be jogged more easily if your final outline pages are written in your personal

hieroglyphics (note that the idea map requires that it be done by hand). The reason is your memory tends to form a mental picture of the page upon recall—it sees not just the contents, but the visual impression (note how the idea map fits this situation). So here's one case in which neatness doesn't count.

🖊 *Memorize in short sessions.* Three short sessions are better than two long ones any day, especially when memorizing. So struggle through the thing once—take a break—then back to the drawing board. You will not be able to remember it all the second time, of course, but after another break, you'll be amazed at how proficient you are becoming at reproducing it.

🖊 *Memorize Audibly.* You will memorize much faster if you speak the words of the outline aloud as you try to recall them. Just be careful, and don't go wandering around the student center babbling bits and pieces of Gibbon and Locke. You may end up in the psychiatrist's office.

🖊 *Practice Writing.* After you have attempted to recall orally, practice writing the outline or drawing the idea map on a piece of paper. Then check the original, and fill in where you could not remember.

All these helpful hints about memorizing are probably unnecessary. I found memorizing to be no problem at all, and I'm probably the world's worst where photographic memories are concerned. Just read through it, speak it aloud, write it, then try and recall. Take a break and try to recall again, checking for mistakes and omissions. The next time or two should be a charm.

Step 7: Using the outline or map at exam time.

The exam itself should now be a breeze. Most of the questions will trigger instantly the pieces of the master outline or idea map you have studied and mastered. On more difficult questions where the answers are found scattered in bits and pieces throughout the course, use the trigger outline/map as a checklist.

Quickly take a mental run-through, asking yourself at each outline station or idea map branch, "Is anything pertinent here?" It is in these bits and pieces of hard-to-find information that you can add a lot to your score. The name of the game is Quantity. Everyone's going to get two or three facts applicable to the question. But with your mental checklist, you should be able to reach into every nook and cranny of the semester work, piling nugget upon factual nugget, as you exhaust every available means to demonstrate evidence of your grasp of the course.

Finally, the trigger outline/map serves as a marvelous psychological weapon. You're not nearly so likely to choke when you take your place on the academic griddle. Your mind is less likely to go blank when you know that the entire course is there at your fingertips.

The trigger outline/map is also invaluable when answering those occasional "trick questions," in which the answer is buried deep within the factual strata of the course. Or the answer may not be there at all—but must be inferred from other material which was covered. It's in these cases where your mental checklist serves you best. While others are groping in the statistical wilderness, you are zipping through your trigger outline/map, asking "Is it here?" or "What about this section? Is it in any way relevant?" I tell you, it works every time! This method, coupled with the tactical suggestions outlined in Chapters 14-21, should get you through the exam with enough gold nuggets to buy your weight in grade points.

Chapter Summary

1. Essay tests require memorizing facts.

2. Learn to highlight/outline/idea map to develop a master outline or map of assigned material for class.

3. Complete the outline or map in class.

4. In preparation for the test, memorize the trigger outline/map.

13

Contents under Pressure

How to Cram Your Way to Graduation

n old wives' tale has been circulating around for some time that condemns cramming as the supreme "no, no." Do it and you will get warts or something to that effect!

Those who perpetuate this ridiculous myth are usually aged professors who harbor the noble delusion that the good student is one whose craving for knowledge is so strong that he or she has no need for concentrated review. On the other hand, they believe that students are just beginning to study at the cram session, in which case failure is imminent.

This is sheer nonsense. The student who doesn't cram, but relies on his day-to-day absorption, can rarely expect to excel, no matter how interested or dedicated he or she may be. Such students may come to know more about the subject than class competitors five years in the future, but at exam time, those who burn the midnight oil hold the aces.

Cramming is like putting carbonated water into a seltzer bottle. The more fizz you force into the bottle, the greater will be the discharge on release. Conversely, the longer the seltzer sits in the bottle, the less potent it becomes. Likewise, the more time you leave those facts and figures deteriorating away in your think tank, the more difficult it will be to extract them from the cobwebs. Instead of bursting forth spontaneously at your summons, you'll have to dig for those facts—laboriously excavating for every precious gift—and separate the relevant data from the chaff of bygone memorabilia.

The guy or gal who goes out the night before a quiz, rationalizing that they "kept up all semester," is only kidding him- or herself. He or she is like the prizefighter who trains for months, then elects to "knock off" the day or two before the championship bout.

This is not to say that you should begin your study the night before. The repetition principle underlies the fact that studying will be easier and retention greater if you break study time into a number of sessions. However, that final evening session is the most important of them all. Facts and figures dissipate with time, and the quickest fades are in the first few hours after exposure.

Never underestimate the value of that last-minute "booster shot." It not only boosts, but it also instills knowledge long forgotten or never absorbed.

The Final Cramdown

The most important moments you'll spend studying are those twelve hours or so before the exam. It's too late at this point for any more actual learning. Henceforth, time must be spent in organizing your thoughts for instantaneous recall. The testing room, remember, is nothing more than an academic vomitorium, where material already digested is regurgitated for the professor's inspection.

The main goal now is to strengthen your ability to recollect the "trigger outline/map" discussed in the preceding chapter. If you can just assemble those bones at the proper time, the "flesh" will take hold automatically.

After you have finished the initial memorization (see Chapter 12), be sure your last task before you turn in for the night and your first task in the morning before you even brush your teeth is to go over the trigger outline or map. A quick review of the master outline/map is also a good idea in order to make fitting the flesh to the bones easier, if you've got the time. On awakening, try to recall it from start to finish. It may not be easy the first time, but strain to wring out every piece possible from the gray matter. Only after you are sure you cannot possibly remember any more should you consult the written outline.

During your shower, run through it again, aloud this time (nobody will hear you with the water running). Keep reviewing it in your mind as you dress, eat breakfast, and even while you drive to campus. Remember the repetition rule: Retention and recall increase with each brief cram session—and those last-minute exposures are the most vivid of all!

Chapter Summary

1. Plan to cram prior to every test. It's like a booster shot.

2. Organize thoughts for instantaneous recall.

3. Use the distributed learning (practice with rest breaks) to connect with the trigger outline or map.

PART FOUR

THE WAR IS ON

Part Four Introduction
The War is On

Eight Tricky Tips Your Teacher Never Taught You

True or False ...?

T or F Eat a good, hearty meal before taking the exam; This will give you strength to overcome fatigue.

T or F There is no need to think about what will be on the exam once in the testing room. It is time now to concentrate on relaxing and overcoming your tension.

T or F Read through the exam quickly before you begin to write. Some questions may trigger answers to others that you are not quite sure about.

T or F If you can't answer a question, move on to the next one and forget about it. Chances are if you don't know it on first go-around, further concentration will not help.

**Secret No. 5
Making Tests
Count**

If you answered "True" to any of the above, consider yourself hoodwinked. It is a great probability that you are one of those students who lose a minimum of five or ten points on every exam.

Believe it or not, passing exams is not all about studying! There are many testing techniques used to transmit the learned material from brain to paper, which are almost as important as study, but way easier to cash in on. The eight examples of academic chicanery outlined in this section are baubles to be cherished and utilized. Read and re-read them until they are firmly embedded in your mind and are easily accessible when the need arises.

14

Tip No. 1

Eat Your Way to Success

Scientific studies have shown that *what you eat does make a difference* in your exam score. In such studies, students with comparable IQ's and grade averages took exams simultaneously. These students took the same class under the same teacher and were tested over identical material.

One group was instructed to eat a light lunch before the exam, which was scheduled for early afternoon. The other group banqueted on steak and potatoes, followed by a mouth-watering array of tempting desserts.

The results were incredible! The "light lunchers" scored at least twenty-five percent higher than the chow hounds in every case!

The reason for this is fairly simple. The body works overtime in digesting food—pulling blood and energy from the brain, causing the machinery in the think tank to bog down. The obvious tip here is to eat a snack and only a snack before each exam, which will increase your ability to remember and focus, while you encourage your epicurean classmates to have another helping! As for yourself, reserve the big meals on exam days for celebration after the fact on your job well done!

Chapter Summary

1. What you eat does affect your exam score.
2. Eat lightly.

15

Tip No. 2

An Easy Technique to Help You Remember under Pressure

Ever stop to consider the bizarre ritual that takes place whenever those exam questions are distributed? It is almost as if the Angel of Death were moving ominously among the populace, passing out doomsday cards.

As the exam begins, crinkling flurry pierces the stillness as a hundred nervous fingers whirl through the test pages, seeking some kind of assurance. Here and there, little sighs and groans signify the lowering of the curve.

The drama continues: pencils break; bladders fill. A sudden crackling of papers indicates that a portion of the class has finished the first page. Those still on page one are panic-stricken, the tension mounting. Someone asks the teacher a question and all ballpoints screech to a halt as every ear strains for clues.

As the period nears its close, the victims begin transporting their scribbled or bubbled offerings toward the desk of judgment. A somber proclamation that "time's up!" ushers in the final agony. Once again, the little murmurs of gasps and groans emit from the mouths of those not quite ready to seal their fates. As the papers rattle and the chairs screech, the stupefied diehards clatter out into the hall where the verbal autopsy roars hot and heavy.

Such needless melodrama…

With a few simple techniques, you can avoid this entire burdensome hullabaloo and emerge from the fiery furnace tried but triumphant. Here's how: As you arrive at the testing room, the condemned will be huddled together in the hallway, waiting for the ax to fall. Resist all urges to unite with this plaintive assembly—it has nothing to offer but group frustration.

Instead, pass right on by the Wailing Wall and go directly into the testing room to stake out your seat—that very same one where you will sit to take the exam. There, in the last few moments before the time begins, put the wheels in motion for a little academic trickery that may later prove invaluable should you hit a mental snag while taking the exam.

We all have those little mental blocks, or "brain farts" as they are most commonly referred to, and they can be costly. The usual procedure is to continue with the test and come back later in the hopes the memory will somehow jog in the meantime. This technique too often fails, however, and it frequently results in serious time problems. Once absorbed in any form of a question, it will behoove you to complete it right then and there, if at all possible, before moving on to another section. You may always return to take another whack at it, if the time allotment so allows after the rest of the test has been completed. The "I'll come back later gag" too often backfires, so if not so much as a simple attempt is made on the initial sweep, you will have lost your chance to receive any credit at all.

In my early college career, I formulated a little system for dealing with these mental blocks. While others were fluttering about, exchanging fears and condolences, I quietly retreated to the seat I had selected for taking the test. There, I reviewed my trigger outline/idea map and master outline/idea map if time permitted. Later, when I hit a snag on the test, I simply put down my pencil and went back in my mind to when I first walked into the room, selected a seat, and had last gone over my material, reviewing the trigger and master outlines/maps. Would you believe that, in roughly seventy percent of the cases, the lost material would flash to mind almost immediately!

The principle behind this bit of magic is simple. Ever forget something you were supposed to do and, try as you might, you could not possibly seem to remember? Perhaps you found that if you returned to the spot where the idea or suggestion last occurred to you, you would suddenly remember. Psychologists call this phenomenon "Recall by Association." It works just as well in retrieving facts on exams as it does in remembering whom to telephone or what groceries to buy. I realized quickly that if I reviewed my notes in the seat I chose for the test, I could nearly always get instant recall back at that same location. By using this method, you have gained a "head start close" on the throng of scared students clustered outside in the hallway. Unlike them, you will not need that five to ten minute adjustment to get into the study mood; you're already in it when the test begins!

Chapter Summary

1. Get to the testing site early and get the best seat possible.

2. Review your trigger outline/map and master outline/map just before the test begins. It helps break mental blocks using "Recall by Association."

3. Once you start an essay question, finish it.

16

Tip No. 3

No Peeking

I t is a crucial moment when the test questions are finally passed out. After days of blind preparation, the veil is suddenly lifted and the true nature of the beast is revealed.

Let the sound of crackling papers serve to remind you: Do not go zipping anxiously through the questions in a harried attempt to satisfy that aching curiosity. Here is what happens when you do: Question 1 is easy (it usually is). You feel pretty sure you can answer it. Question 2 is so-so. Maybe with a little bluffing you can pull it off. Suddenly, your eyes fasten on Question 3—the shark tooth among the seashells! It's a bugger, obviously calculated to separate the Fulbrights from the flunkys. And sure enough, all the time you're grappling with Questions 1 and 2 (the easy ones, remember), your brain cells are concentrating on Question 3.

Avoid this little pitfall by *refusing to read through the exam before attempting to answer the questions.* The aged philosophy propounded by many educators that a question down the line may spark an earlier answer is a spurious one. Occasionally, in an objective quiz, one question may betray an answer to another. In such a case, it is an easy matter to turn back and make the change. On the other hand, essay questions are usually pretty well divided as to pertinence. Looking ahead is much more apt to hinder rather than help. Don't do it!

Besides, when you do get down to Question 3 and apply all of your energies to it, including that oh-so-valuable mental checklist, you may find you can come up with the answer after all. By that time, you will have amassed full credit on Questions 1 and 2. So assume from the moment the questions are passed out that you can answer them all—and proceed to do just that.

Chapter Summary

1. When you receive the test, allocate time to each question or section.

2. Leave time for review.

3. Read the question only when you are ready to answer it.

17

Tip No. 4

How Not to Get Caught with Your Pants Down

ust as misguided as the person who reads all the questions before the test begins, is the individual who swings too far the other way.

As soon as the exam sheet is passed out, the writing utensil clicks into action and he or she charges boldly into the fray, vigorously churning out pages upon pages of illegible cuneiform just as fast as their squiggling fingers can transport them. This ill-fated scholar is usually still happily barreling through Question 2 when the ten-minute warning sounds to signal impending doom. The student who knew too much has hanged himself by his own cacographic scrawl.

The first thing one should do when those test questions are distributed is to *time the exam.* Count (not read) the exam questions to allot so much time to each. If certain questions are weighted more heavily, it is probable that those questions contain more veiled answers than the others (and not necessarily that the question is harder). So take this into consideration when apportioning time.

In addition, *be sure to leave at least ten minutes* at the end of the exam as a safety margin. You will constantly run the risk of exceeding your time limits so keep those precious few minutes in reserve, just in case. You can always use them to go back and clean up misspelled words and sloppy sentences or make sure your Scantron is correctly filled out, though you will find this luxury is rarely afforded.

Remember, you may know more than anyone else in the class, but unless you get it down on paper, you might just as well not know a thing. As tempting as it seems, do not elaborate too much (unless you honestly don't know and are just trying to fill space). After all, you are not trying to teach the grader anything— you only want to let him or her know how much you know and how well you understand it. Once you have made it clear that you understand a point, move on to another one, without rambling on unnecessarily. Some teachers will even express before the first test that they do not wish to read countless paragraphs of irrelevant or nonpertinent information. Such teachers usually advise you to write down only what sufficiently proves the answer to the question at hand, even if that means only writing a few sentences. This makes it easier for both of you, as you have more time during the test and the grader gains more free time *after* the test!

Finally, read and reread the question. Carefully consider the instructions to be sure you understand what is being asked. From time to time, during the answering of a question, go back to the quiz sheet and read those instructions over once again—just to make certain you are staying on the right track. A great number of test questions are missed simply because the student failed to comprehend what was being asked.

Be sure you don't lose the race before the shot even sounds to begin it: *Read the instructions!*

Chapter Summary

1. Time the questions in the exam, giving more time for heavier weighted questions and enough time for review.

2. Read and reread the question to be sure you understand.

3. Read the instructions.

18

Tip No. 5

Look Before You Leap

ow many times have you been told to be sure to contemplate a question before putting pencil to paper? How few actually follow this beneficial advice?

Before burning up the Blue Book, set aside the pencil for a moment and carefully consider the question. Perhaps, if time permits, jot down on a piece of paper an idea map or the points you want to cover, running quickly through your mental checklist to be certain that no potential nuggets are overlooked. Then take the bits and pieces on the scratch pad and rearrange them in the most logical order—the order in which they will be discussed. Remember: The professor has dozens of other papers just like yours to grade, and consequently the same answers will pop up again and again. Eventually, the set of papers will tend to become a repetitious blur, so set your paper apart from the others by having it well-organized. A logical, clean presentation is worth a few extra points. Again, competition is the name of the game.

I needn't dwell on the necessity for good penmanship. It stands to reason, if the grader's mind is occupied with deciphering your cryptic hen- scratching, he or she surely will not be overly impressed with the content of your essay.

Chapter Summary

1. Think before you answer; jot down an outline or idea map.
2. Organize your answer to set yourself apart.
3. Write legibly.

19

Tip No. 6

The Importance of Being Shakespeare

Remember what we just recently discussed about setting your essay apart from the competition? Well, here is a little gimmick to distinguish your answers from the mundane blur of facts and figures which the grader will monotonously read over and over again.

Few of us have time to cement all that tedious data together with flowery phrases and descriptive verbiage, à la Noel Coward. We are too obsessed with our primary concern—getting as many facts and figures down as possible—to be concentrating on originality.

The effortless way to sprinkle on a little pixie dust is to have a few stock phrases in your holster before the test gets under way. No time need be spent in coming up with the unusual during exam time, since all your creative thinking has been done beforehand—even months before. A couple of well-chosen gems now can be used over and over again, all through college.

Example:

"Self-confessed criminals should not be permitted to *seek the warm shelter* of the Fifth Amendment."

This little phrase, "seek the warm shelter," popped up again and again on my exam papers. Somebody was always *seeking the warm shelter*: of the myelin sheath over neuronal axons in the brain, or of diplomatic immunity, or of a philosopher's assurance concerning the workings of the world. This little exercise in literary acrobatics required no particular creative effort, and proved exceedingly handy as its applications were amazingly universal. Many were the times when I would get a test paper returned and there, out in the margin opposite my stock phrase, the grader had written "Good!" or "Well put!"

Make up a few colorful phrases of your own. If you are not necessarily the creative type, never fear! *Reader's Digest* has a page full every month, or you can always memorize a few high-quality ones from your outside reading. A scintillating witticism here, a droll phrase or two there, and before you know it, you too may find academic gratification under the *warm shelter* of your own pseudo-literary style.

Warning!

Be sure you do not use the same phrase twice with the same teacher or professor.

Chapter Summary

1. Set yourself apart by being prepared.
2. Memorize a few phrases e.g. "Seek the warm shelter," which can be thrown in at will.
3. Be careful not to use the same phrase twice with the same teacher or professor.

20

Tip No. 7

Ask the Teacher

A dilemma that frequently arises is what to do when you simply are not sure of the answer to a test question. The solution is often easy: Ask the teacher.

No, you did not read wrong. Nervy as it may sound, asking the teacher or professor whether an answer is correct is the most direct means of getting help on an exam, short of simply copying from someone else's paper, a dangerously risky business at best.

Surprisingly, the "ask and it shall be given" technique often achieves phenomenal results. After all, if you've followed the apple-polishing guidelines outlined in Chapter 7, the professor is on your side—he or she wants you to pass!

Of course, you just don't haul your Blue Book or Scantron up to the desk and demand, "What's the answer to No. 7?" You must be a bit more discreet. My favorite ploy is, "I'm not sure what is meant by No. 7 when it says…" You will be amazed how often the teacher or professor will tell you not only what was meant by No. 7, but also what answer to put down! Example (as you stand there looking genuinely puzzled): "Why, don't you remember a couple of weeks ago when we talked about that in class?" A couple of weeks ago you talked about Hannibal's military strategy—so there you have it.

It is absolutely incredible how far a teacher or professor will sometimes go to reveal an answer to a favorite student. One of my best stunts was to take an objective quiz to the front of the room and ask some inane question like, "In Question 3, I assume you mean to apply that question just to the period covered during the last six weeks?" All the while, it's really Question 2 I'm concerned about, where I've already marked an answer. If I've answered it wrong, the professor almost always will volunteer, "Now are you sure about your answer up there in Question 2?" Amazing!

Of course, if the gambit does not work, and it won't about half the time, he will simply say, "I can't say" or "Think about it very carefully." You have lost absolutely nothing in trying. After all, you have only just asked for clarification. But if you've done your apple-polishing, you will often be delighted to find the professor is just as anxious to curry favor with you as you are with him or her!

Chapter Summary

1. When you are in doubt about a question, ask the professor.
2. You will earn a good reply if you've used the apple-polishing techniques in Chapter 7.
3. You may also get a bonus with help on a question already answered.

21

Tip No. 8

Sins of Omission

n objective type exams, it is occasionally profitable to leave a question blank, i.e. when there is a penalty for guessing. In essay exams, never leave a question blank.

Objective quizzes are judged purely on the basis of rights and wrongs. Apple polishing is of little value here. Therefore, all things being equal, it would be best to answer every question, even if you in fact do not know, since a wrong answer will not count any more against you than an omission. However, in recent years, the academic popularity of such innovations as double jeopardy and rights-wrongs has done much to deaden student applause over true-false and multiple-choice questions. Before one goes charging indiscriminately down the page, checking T's and F's with frivolous abandon, it's a good idea to know which grading system is being applied.

In essay exams, there is one superior rule about blank spaces: Don't leave any! Be cautious, however, if the professor has directed students to choose and answer only a certain number of the questions given. In such instances, there is a great chance that one will be penalized for answering more than what is asked. This happens most frequently because the student is not absolutely sure of an answer so he or she answers an extra question half-heartedly just to increase the chances of receiving credit. Conversely, most teachers who ask students to answer only three out of the five given questions, will only grade the first three answered. Therefore, though a student answers the fourth question most confidently, it will go unnoticed or remain ungraded because the directions clearly stated that only the first three answers would be taken into consideration.

Otherwise, the objective to be achieved in essay exams is to create the impression that you know something. A bold omission smack dab in the middle of the Blue Book is a red flag announcing: This joker doesn't know anything! This kind of advertising we can do without. Not only will you get zero credit for the question left out, but also the stigma of stupidity attaches immediately and you remain haunted by it for the rest of the exam. ("If the dullard didn't know a thing about Question 2, he can't know much about Question 3 either...") So, if at all possible, get some plausible answer down for every question on the test.

This isn't always easy, particularly if you know absolutely nothing pertaining to the query. Instead of putting down some whimsical gobbledygook, which will be immediately recognized as just that, try this: Put down the answer to another question—one you *can* answer. If the professor asks you for the causes of the Japanese war and you don't know, list the causes of the Siamese war—and label it as such: "The causes of the Siamese war are..."

Now, rather than advertising your complete lack of knowledge, you've only demonstrated your failure to read the question correctly— a minor sin by comparison. You will still be counted off, of course, but now, instead of that aura of stupidity dogging your tracks for the remainder of the test, the professor or grader may actually be feeling a wee bit sorry for you. ("Gee, it's too bad about old Charlie/Charlene misreading that question....") He or she may even feel a little guilty about having to count the question wrong, and will unconsciously try to compensate for your mistake by grading just a bit more leniently from there on out.

So, remember this gimmick if you are ever at a loss. Misread the question on purpose as one to which you *do* know the answer. I have seen it work on a number of occasions. After all, nobody would actually have the nerve to pull that kind of tomfoolery, now would they?

Chapter Summary

1. Never leave an essay question blank.
2. If you don't have a clue to the answer, then answer a question you do know as if you misread the original question.

PART FIVE

Grim Reapers I Have Known

Part Five Introduction
Grim Reapers I Have Known

They are called the Big Six, otherwise known as: (1) freshman English, (2) foreign languages, (3) math, (4) public speaking, (5) terms, themes/papers, and (6) finals. On the surface, the title may seem to be overkill. Yet, each one is feared in much the same way. In fact, as a case in point, some people have chosen the grim reaper over public speaking.

In the chapters to come, we will discuss a method of attack to put your mind at ease. You will find suggestions concerning preparation, so the reality will not be as shocking. The more convincing the rationale, the more successful the preparation, the less challenging the Big Six will be.

If the processes outlined in the chapters are even partially successful, I predict that in certain instances, you will see the Big Six as an opportunity of a lifetime.

Read on, my friends. Help is on the way!

22

Freshman English

As soon as you open your mouth, or put thoughts on paper, your words and the way you use them will paint a picture of you. At times, you may be seen as a buffoon; at others, as a reasonably well-educated person. As a result, most high schools and colleges require that every incoming student either test out of or take freshman English; and for good reason. As one sage observed, "It is far better to say nothing and be thought a fool, than to open one's mouth and remove all doubt." He could have been talking about someone who could not pass English 101.

Your English will serve you well for the rest of your life, or become a millstone around your neck wherever you go. Even your vocabulary will open doors for you; or, on the other hand, betray you. In fact, one indicator of intelligence is the size and variety of a person's vocabulary. For these reasons, the study of English and its attendant facets should be seen as a real opportunity to excel. Excitement and eagerness should accompany the study of this subject. In such light, it would behoove you to improve your vocabulary on a regular basis. As a start, use the

Word Power section in *Reader's Digest*, or go back and look up the definitions of words you did not understand in a recent book you were reading.

While the ability to turn a phrase is an art, a number of mechanics must be mastered. The novice should discover how to analyze the audience and write in a way to interest those for whom the material is intended, as well as to satisfy specific purposes. Also, the budding author should learn to dissect the writing into workable units, and become proficient at providing the requirements for specific written assignments. He or she must learn how to draft, revise, and edit written material. In addition, they should strive to master creative writing. All of the above will prepare one to communicate well, because we will spend the rest of our lives doing so by the spoken or written word.

The business world has clearly realized the necessity of correct English. It demands that the computer not only spell check, but also highlight incorrect grammar and syntax. Imagine the humiliation that results when a person is not able to correct a mistake that has been pointed out. Lack of the ability to use English properly has undoubtedly delayed many a promotion or even prevented employment of a job-seeker.

For the reasons above, we cannot overemphasize the importance of English. Do not make the mistake of treating the subject as something to get through as quickly as possible. Instead, view it as a treasure chest. Even if you could succeed in testing out of the requirement, it will be worth your while to take the course with a plan to become even better. In later life, it will be too late to discover that grammar is not only important but can be embarrassing if violated even in everyday conversation.

Look at freshman English as a key to open the doors to higher grade point averages. In the course of your four to eight years of undergraduate and graduate studies, you'll be facing a large number of essay questions in tests, themes, term papers, research briefs, and theses. In your study of English, learn the differences that make up each type of paper. Find out the tricks of the trade in composing each one.

Take time to become computer literate in the specific area of resources. Discover where and how to access the information you will need to produce a paper that will get you top marks. Start by becoming acquainted with the academic databases provided by most campus library systems. Having the right attitude about obtaining and learning the information others take for granted will put you at the head of the class. Recognize immediately that anything worthwhile will take work, and work is never quick nor is it easy.

When in English class, show a desire to go far beyond just what is required to pass the course. Anyone can do that, and most students do just that— pass the course. In your case, English is one opportunity where you must get the professor to provide you with challenges that will raise you head and shoulders above the run-of-the-mill. The written material you produce will be the beacon that puts you in the limelight. Don't let it flash over your head. To put that another way, if you were required to select only one elective course in your entire four years at college, English should be at the top of your list.

Chapter Summary

1. Your words and usage will paint a picture of you.

2. One indication of intelligence is vocabulary. Learn new words.

3. Learn writing mechanics: audience analysis, creative writing, drafting, revision, and editing.

4. Writing is important to business.

5. Learn to use the computer to discover resources.

6. Writing helps to improve one's GPA.

23

Foreign Languages-
It's Greek to Me, Too

magine being stranded in a foreign country and desperately needing to communicate a message, such as, "I need to find a hospital" or "one more beer, please," but no one spoke English. A second language is important, because with one you double the probability of finding someone with whom to communicate. Many other considerations should be broached before making a decision about foreign languages. If a doctorate is even remotely possible in your future, a second language may be a requirement. On the other hand, you could become intrigued by the thought of spending a semester studying abroad. Being able to speak and understand to some degree would be a distinct advantage, not to mention that it would make the experience that much richer.

When to start

Learning any foreign language is best done at an early age. That being said, language training cannot start too early. Grade school will provide an opportunity to become familiar with foreign languages and determine personal preference. High school should be a time when counselors advise students to consider their plans for college in selecting the foreign language they want to study. That way they can continue with the same language in college and ultimately be ready for two semesters in a foreign country, and/ or the requirement of a second language in pursuing a doctorate.

The choice

By college level, a decision as to which language to stick with must be reached. Even if mistakes were made in earlier years, then the next four years are still the most important. When searching to find which language is perfect for you, personal preference should be the key determining factor. If you like being able to speak a particular language, everything about learning it becomes easier.

Keep in mind that anyone can learn if he or she chooses. Consider the story about a father who took his young daughter to learn to speak Polish. After eight weeks had gone by, the father went to the classroom for a progress report. An emotional teacher exclaimed to him that it was utterly impossible to teach his daughter to speak Polish. The father looked at the teacher and said, "Thank goodness she wasn't born in Poland." Then, deciding that his ancestors' language just might not be her forte, he enrolled his daughter in French classes. Now, *Beauty and the Beast* was her absolute favorite movie, of which she had memorized all the songs, including one entitled "Bonjour." Also, the most intriguing character in her eyes was Lumière, the candlestick, who often spoke to the beautiful heroine Belle in French. For this reason, his little girl was most excited to learn this language, and was able to string together simple sentences within eight weeks! Remember, attitude makes all the difference!

Tips for learning

In the study of languages, at least three major parts must be addressed. The first requires the learning of pronunciation, grammar, syntax, idioms, and so forth, which will be explained and accomplished in the classroom. The second major area is the acquisition of vocabulary, and the third is simply to practice. Here, we will discuss the second major area—vocabulary. It is accomplished by using a process of memorization which differs substantially from that used in the chapter on public speaking.

The method most applicable to language memorization began very early in grade school and is called flashcards. These cards are nothing more than the familiar three-by-five cards. Buy a good quantity of three-by-five note cards because they are readily available, sized appropriately, and carried easily. Generally, three processes are used in learning: verbal, aural, and tactile. Most people prefer one method in the learning process, but all three are used from time to time. To capitalize on this fact, we will suggest all three when preparing flashcards.

Suppose you have twenty-five vocabulary words to memorize for the next class. Take a three-by-five card and write the first word on the card, using block letters. Include the definition of the word if appropriate. While doing this, say the word out loud. Then turn the card over and print out the word's equivalent in the foreign language. Again, say everything you write out loud as you are accomplishing the task. Notice that you have used all three learning methods: verbal, (saying the word), aural, (hearing the word), and, tactile (writing it). Continue the process until you have a flashcard for each of the twenty-five words.

Memorizing

Let's use the German language in our example. Go through the list, English to German, by first looking at the word or phrase in English as you say it aloud. You would be using two of the three methods of learning, verbal and aural. Guess what the word or phrase is in German. Check your accuracy. Continue that process for about a half hour. At that point, take a break. Do something else, such as reading, or studying some other subject. After about a half hour return to your memorization task. This time, complete the process by looking at the German side of the flashcards. Continue to check for accuracy. Duplicate this process until you have learned or memorized all of the words or phrases. Should you have trouble with a particular word or phrase, get a piece of scrap paper and write it out. You will be giving yourself the opportunity to use the third one of the three learning methods, tactile.

When possible, try to use the word or phrase in a simple sentence—subject, verb, and object. Another technique in the learning of languages is to study with someone else. That way you can also socialize and laugh. When you are having fun, learning is much easier, faster and more lasting. In that context, try setting an alarm clock. Agree that for a specific time period the two of you will communicate only in the foreign language. You will be amazed at your motivation to learn! The whole language process becomes meaningful. The caveat for language is: use it or lose it.

Chapter summary

1. Study a foreign language. You may need it in later life.

2. It is easier to learn languages early in life.

3. Grammar, syntax and idioms are learned in the classroom; vocabulary is memorized.

4. Use flashcards to learn vocabulary.

5. Learn to say simple sentences in the foreign language.

6. For language, use it or lose it.

24

Math - Fighting Figures

We have thus far talked mostly about the verbal aspect of high school and college courses. Of equal importance is the quantitative portion, or math. Just the thought of math and its many forms turns some people off and others on. Mathematics is universally applicable to our world because it teaches people to think and reason well, while providing an understanding that will lead to more effective decisions.

For most students, their curriculum of choice will dictate which math courses such as algebra, trigonometry, calculus, geometry, and/or statistics they must take. Some of those courses will be prerequisites for Science and Engineering, Computer Technology, Health Sciences, and so forth. Students in other areas of study will find math prerequisites more obscure. Generally speaking, if your chosen major leads to some form of business, you will be required to do calculations, compare relationships, and handle money matters. A course or several courses in math may be essential. Talk specifically about such future needs with your high school or college counselor.

When selecting math courses to study, keep in mind that the various courses tend to build on each other, and that prerequisites are usually required before you are admitted. Review the course offering with your counselor to ensure that the material covered will be useful and applicable to the needs you have. Practically everyone will eventually have to know the budgeting process, how to reconcile their monthly bank statement, and amortize their home mortgage or automobile purchases. More specifically, and crucial to one's future, is the knowledge of how to handle monetary means. Much is to be learned in the broad areas of credit and investments, simple and compound interest, and savings. A wise person once said, "It is not how much money you make, but how much money you keep."

Once you have signed up for a math class, the fun begins. Execute all those beneficial strategies we discussed earlier, such as meeting with the professor ahead of time, learning what will be expected, how the testing procedure will go, and what attendant material would be helpful.

From the beginning, it is most important to understand that almost all, if not all, math material sections will build on top of one another on a class by class basis. What that means is you must know and understand each element, because the next factor will assume the understanding of the previous component, and will add to or build upon it. It further suggests that if you miss a class, you must learn what was covered in that class. Trying to add another element without the previous one would make no sense because the constituent for building purposes is missing.

How to study for math

The methodology I am about to describe for studying in math courses is applicable for the most part in all courses, but especially in the areas of mathematics. Be prepared to attend your classes, meaning you will have to carefully read the textbook chapters to be discussed in class. Try to understand the course material without benefit of the professor's having to explain it. Use a highlighter or underline the key thoughts. Go back and make an outline/idea map of the major concepts, leaving an additional blank sheet. This outline/map should be in front of you during class. You can add comments from the professor's lecture and thus produce a far more comprehensive set of notes.

Usually in the books for math courses there are practice questions or problems to work at the end of the chapters; some are easy and some are more difficult. Do the easy ones, per the example used in the beginning of the chapter. Following that, try the more difficult ones to see if you have mastered the process. Having accomplished the aforementioned, you are ready to attend class. Notice that at class you will be hearing the lesson for the *second* time. You will also be able to ask questions about the more difficult practice problems which may have you currently stumped. Of equal importance, notice how you will impress the professor with questions and an understanding which far exceeds that of the other class members. Such attitude, interest, and brightness can't help but put you in a favorable light,.

Warning! In math courses, it is not so much the ability to get the right answers to problems, but rather the ability to understand what happened to bring about the result obtained. Simply put: *Most important is the ability to understand the lines of reasoning required to justify the end result.* Knowledge to that extent allows one to get the appropriate end result and understand why an answer was correct, enabling you to duplicate the process on later exams.

Tips for studying math

We have thus far entreated you to prepare for class, and to take excellent notes during class. We suggested that you copy them over neatly right after class as a way of repeating the essential material three times:

1. Preparing for class
2. Listening and taking notes during the class
3. Copying your notes legibly right after class

One critical reason for such an approach is that professors will often formulate test questions not only from the textbook, but also from material presented during class. The above strategy is most helpful for courses in which you are having particular comprehension problems and courses where the previous class concepts are expanded upon in each successive class. Be sure to allocate a suitable amount of study time to each class. Our rule of thumb is: *Two to three hours of study for each hour of class time.*

Recognize that studying for a math class differs somewhat from most other classes. In math, you will have both the memorization of rules and formulas along with the solving of problems, and a logic or reasoning component. When one understands the rationale that produces the desired outcome, the lesson has been learned.

Because of this reasoning component, you should have a study buddy or small study group. Though deluding oneself may be simple, convincing others of a wrong conclusion is far more difficult.

Prepare yourself for the change from high school to college. Concerning courses you have previously been introduced to at the high school level, in college you will notice that the content will be broader, deeper, and presented at a much faster rate. You will suddenly find yourself responsible for far more material than you were accustomed to in the past.

By the same token, do not be surprised if your homework in math courses is not collected. In many instances, the actual completion of the assignment will not be considered in the determination of your final grade, but the failure to attempt these tasks or the achievement of them will surely become apparent.

Chapter Summary

1. Math helps you think and reason.

2. Math courses build on each other; check prerequisites.

3. Be prepared for your classes by outlining/mapping the assigned materials and working the practice problems.

4. Understanding the process is as equally important as getting the right answer.

5. Add to your notes in the subsequent class.

6. Study with a small group to check the reasoning component of math courses.

25

Public Speaking

A survey was taken that asked people what they feared most. Surprisingly, some respondents rated public speaking more terrifying than death! One possible reason is in death you die once, but in public speaking, you can die a thousand times, so to speak. The only way to conquer that panic is to tear it apart and examine it.

Why speech is important

We will talk first about the benefits of public speaking. The ability to stand up and present your thoughts in a clear, concise, and convincing manner will have immeasurable payoffs. Earlier we spoke about class discussion, and how it could add significantly to your final grade if done well. Think about these possibilities: Some of your classes will require a project to be accomplished and then presented to the class. The whole assignment could account for half the final grade. You might choose to run for a class office that would require many talks at student gatherings.

If you hold an office in a fraternity, sorority, social club, or one of a hundred special-interest groups, speaking will be required.

Eventually, you will have to interview for a job. Whether you are in a one-on-one situation, or one to a small group, the same speaking principles will apply. In all of the speaking occasions outlined above, you will have the opportunity to do well or at least better than average. Success will depend greatly on your speaking performance.

Preparation

Speaking is an art, and you cannot start training too early. Grade school exposure to speaking would be best, but be sure that you take one or more speech courses while in high school. At that level, you will be taught the important fundamentals and be expected to make mistakes as you learn. If possible, participate in the high school class play each year. As you progress through these four years of high school, you can expect to be selected for longer speaking parts. Ideally, get on the high school debate team. Nothing can provide you a better experience. View speaking as a challenge that will pay increasingly handsome dividends.

Without fail, take a public speaking course in college. You will be spending the rest of your life speaking in some way, shape, or form. If time permits, you may be able to join the college debate team. If you have ample elective hours, consider an introductory course in drama.

Assuming that the closest you will get to a public speaking course is this book, we will acquaint you with the basics.

Posture

As our parents have always said, "Stand up straight with your shoulders back." When you are not gesturing, let your arms hang down at your sides naturally. Walk slowly in front of your audience if your microphone cord will allow or if you are not impeded by one. Look your audience in the eyes as you scan. Should that prove too difficult, pick three people, one in the middle and one to either side, to fixate on as you scan your audience.

Enunciation, Volume, and Pace

Learn to speak clearly and distinctly. You may have to practice with a mouth full of pebbles as did the Greek philosopher, Demosthenes; though to be safe, use marshmallows instead. You must produce sufficient volume to be heard by your intended audience. Learn how to project your voice. It is said people can listen to and comprehend four times faster than the normal person speaks. I recommend you learn to speak about twice as fast as you normally speak. In that manner, your audience will still be able to listen to and comprehend twice as fast, and therefore, will not become bored as quickly. On occasion use inflexion and silence. They are like salt and pepper. Though, if you pull a Jackie Chan and the audience cannot understand the words that are coming out of your mouth, then all is lost!

Material

Until you become a master at impromptu remarks, write out what you want to say, word for word. It takes about two minutes to say what is typed on a double spaced 8 1/2 x 11 sheet of paper. Wherever possible, use stories to illustrate your point. People remember the stories and thereby remember the point.

Always start out with a statement, story, fact, or pronouncement to startle or pique the interest of your listener. Example: "Did you know that today one hundred twenty-six people will die in car accidents somewhere in the United States of America? And that forty of them would have survived had they been wearing a seat belt." Use the body of your material to state your case in a logical sequence. Cite the opinions of experts to corroborate your position. Develop what you want the reader to do. Example: You must make buckling your seat belt a habit by doing it every time you are in a car. Challenge them to act because the outcomes are so rewarding. End your material with another shocking piece of information. Example, "I hope that I have convinced you to buckle your safety belt because, you see, I am one of those who survived an accident. My seat belt was buckled." Remember, gaining the trust of the audience is key to any successful speech, and the more proof you provide and the better your sources, the more credible you seem.

Reading It

In some instances, you will be able to read your material to the audience. Preparing for such means having it typed double-spaced and underlined at places of emphasis. Practice reading your material enough times so that you need only to glance at a sentence to say it while looking at your audience. Then glance again at the paper, and after using your finger to locate your place, look up and continue your presentation.

Memorization

At other times, you may have to memorize your material. Our memories are like a muscle. The more you exercise them, the stronger they become. To commit to memory a piece of material, you must first separate it into ten or twenty key thoughts. These primary points should be represented by a triggering word or phrase. At this point, I must digress to explain the House of Hooks memory method. If you walk into my kitchen, you would see a table with four chairs, a picture on the wall, a small TV, a baker's rack, toaster oven, a coffee maker, cabinets, sinks, refrigerator, oven, range, microwave, and a telephone. Each one of these is a hook, and I can recall them by mentally walking through the kitchen. I then tie each keyword or phrase to each appliance.

Example:

In our story above, let's say one hundred twenty-six people were killed in car accidents. Picture in your mind the kitchen table with the number 126 sitting on it, or 126 bodies piled on the table. Further, suppose forty of them did not have seat belts on. They are piled on the four chairs. Continue through the story, and hook the keywords or phrases to remaining kitchen furnishings. If you run out of hooks, go into the family room and start over. As you present the material, you mentally walk through your kitchen and the keywords or phrases will trigger what you want to talk about.

As you prepare to memorize, keep in mind that you should use the Distributed Trials method. In other words, after you established the hooks using your dorm room or whatever room you are intimately familiar with, tie the key- words or key phrases to them. Then run through a trial to see what accuracy you have. After three trials, pause and participate in another activity. Study some other subject, read a book, or watch TV for a half hour. Return to the task of memorizing your material and go through a few trials, always checking your accuracy. Take another break and do something else. Repeat that process a few times and you will soon be successful!

General Ideas

When speaking publicly, be sure that your attitude is upbeat. You have to be excited and convinced that what you have to say is both important and worthwhile to hear. Remember to smile at your audience! If something is extremely funny, laugh with the audience. They want to know that you are having a good time, too. If you are positive, it will psychologically set you to remember far more effortlessly and to do a drastically better job.

Postgraduate Work

For those who want even more training, there is an association called Toastmasters. The organization's approach is to meet as a group once a week, and go through activities to continually improve public speaking. They have chapters that meet for breakfast, lunch, dinner, and probably at other times, with the sole purpose of becoming excellent public speakers. The cost is minimal, and the outcomes are spectacular! Learn the tricks of public speaking, and it will serve you well in ways you cannot even begin to imagine.

Chapter Summary

1. Public speaking will be used throughout life and will pay handsome dividends.

2. Start your learning process early; do high school debate; be a part of the school play.

3. Watch your posture; use clear and distinct speech; project your voice.

4. Use room hooks to memorize.

5. Build interest at the start; follow with the body of material; use a clever ending.

6. Join Toastmasters for further training.

26

Term Themes and Papers - Buy Yourself an A

During your high school and college years and in more than one course, a paper of some sort will be assigned. It may be called by any one of a number of titles, such as: term paper, theme, essay, research paper, or thesis. These papers will generally represent a large portion of your final grade. The reason professors think so highly of these written efforts rests in the fact that such assignments give you a chance to shine, especially if you are one of those who do not perform well on tests, for whatever reason.

In writing papers, you can usually take as much time as necessary, because you can start early and work late into the night, if you so choose. Furthermore, you will be able to show off your investigative prowess. Perhaps you could find little-known sources that could possibly add to the field. By the same token, you may have

**Secret No. 6
Idea Map
Your Papers
for Creativity**

acquired the Internet knowledge to scour the World Wide Web for everything you want to know about the assigned subject or the one you have selected. Even more importantly, you will have the opportunity to acquaint the reader or grader with your ability to think, to offer proofs of your position, to dismantle known objections to your point, to gain credibility, and ultimately to prevail in presenting your thesis.

When such assignments are announced, a number of groans and sighs will come from the class-at-large. Do not let them phase you in the least, for you have just been given the opportunity of a lifetime. Start immediately to develop a plan to produce a paper that will give you the GPA you wish to obtain.

Step 1

Be absolutely sure you clearly understand all of the requirements as given in the assignment. Even if the professor puts it in writing and hands it out, pay most attention to the professor's added comments and caveats as he or she goes through what will be expected. Should you have a question, ask it at that time. Two reasons for asking immediately are:

- ❖ Most likely, a number of other students have the same question.
- ❖ You will avoid immediately charging off in the wrong direction.

Step 2

Create an outline of the paper to be written. Use an idea map in working with the subject of your paper as shown in Chapter 7. To digress for a moment, recognize that in Chapter 7 you were idea mapping a chapter in a book for the purpose of memorization. When idea mapping your paper, in one sense, you are doing the reverse. Keep in mind that the right side of our brain does not think in a linear fashion. Hence, we left brain-dominant people waste time not knowing where to start. For this assigned paper, start immediately by simply drawing an oval on a piece of paper. Write the topic in the oval. Draw a few lines radiating from the center oval and add an oval at the end of each one. As you think of major points supporting the topic, list them in the ovals. Draw shorter lines jutting off from the major lines, like tree branches. When the mind sees blank lines, the right or creative side of our brain has a tendency to fill in the blanks. So, as you get a major idea, write it on one of the ovals. Minor ideas would go on the shorter lines. Draw a circle around the idea branches that go together. Arrange these major groups in rank order by sequence, importance, logicality. You are now ready to write.

The following was adapted, with permission from *Business Writing that Counts,* by Dr. Julie Miller. You will see an idea map showing the process for producing the material necessary for writing papers. In general, when creating the paper, your opening thoughts should be the thesis or objective of the work. It will set the stage for all of the writing. Next, indicate what sources you will find to bolster your position and possibly what objections you will dispel. Finally, show your summary and conclusions.

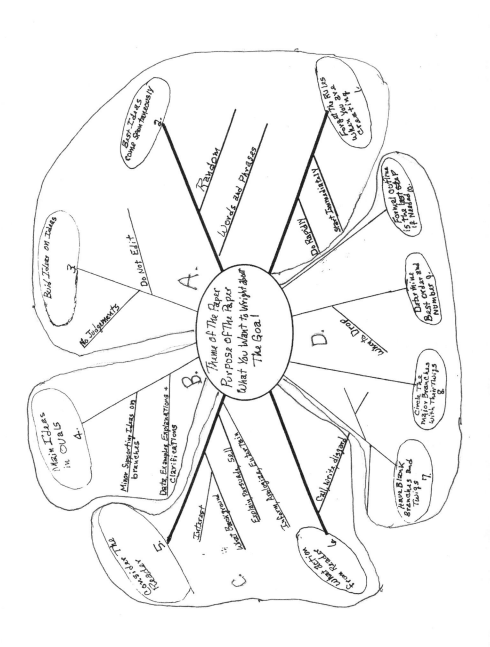

Step 3

Make an appointment with your professor or T.A for the purpose of discerning at this early juncture whether you are about to step off in the wrong direction or if you are right on track. Nothing could be more important than this step. You can be sure that they will be most willing to keep you from making a colossal mistake. Often they will be helpful in sharpening your focus, should you be slightly off mark. While there, converse with them about the sources you intend to use. I had a professor warn me about a source that would have muddied the waters and he actually suggested one, unknown to me, that turned out to be a major contributor to the paper's excellence. Recognize that this step is actually paving the way with the person who will ultimately grade the paper. It is not likely he or she would grade down something that they had a hand in creating!

When actually writing the paper, use the conventional format as required by your type of paper and school or college you are attending. If completely in the dark on format, or this is your first exposure, use Step 3 again. The professor or TA will know some source that can be used to bone up on the basics.

Once you have completed the paper, never take the first attempt as final. In freshman English, you will have learned how to edit your work. If some of your phrasing sounds stilted to you, it probably is. Rephrase that portion so any bright high school student would understand it. When in doubt, use shorter words and shorter sentences. Never use a word you do not understand or one you are not likely to ever use again. On the other hand, stray away from using the same word too many times in the same paragraph. Many colleges and universities have a department where you can find assistance when writing papers. If your college has those resources, by all means use them. While those tutors may not be able to judge the accuracy of your sources, or even if they apply to the work you are doing, they can show you how to make your writing flow. With their help, you might be able to turn a B+ paper into an A-. It will certainly be worth the effort to learn how to improve your written proposition.

Realizing that not all papers will account for the same grade percentage, be sure that you are aware of where your paper falls. Obviously, the larger the percentage, the more effort you should expend and the better job you should do. Unfortunately, some students do an equally poor job on all papers. Instead, opt to do a consistently good job on all papers.

Caveats

Be absolutely sure you do not plagiarize material, however tempting it may be. The resulting consequences, such as loss of grade, having to retake the course, and live with the accompanying stigma, are not worth it.

One saving grace about papers is that as you continue to produce them, they will become easier. Admittedly, when you are working on the first four or five papers, such a prediction seems far-fetched, but you can be rest assured it is a true statement. The rationale for that testimonial is based on the fact that you learn with each paper, which positively affects your attitude. Your attitude, in turn, positively sets you to do a better job, thus turning it into a self-fulfilling prophecy.

Chapter Summary

1. Clearly understand the requirements for the paper.

2. Idea map the approach you will take to quicken the process and produce a more complete paper.

3. Meet with the professor or TA concerning the outline to assure the correct direction.

4. Edit the results until you have a final product.

5. Get help if necessary.

27

A Word about Finals

Often the words "It is finals week" strikes terror in the hearts of many students. That does not have to happen, provided you do something about it. The alternative is to do nothing and then to cram the night before tests, which is a sure formula for failure. Note that in this instance, *cram* is not used as the distributed practice process we talked about in Chapter 13. An effective plan starts on the first day of classes and includes givens, such as:

- attend all classes
- complete and turn in all assignments
- outline or idea map the class material
- take additional notes in class
- rewrite the notes legibly after the class
- participate in class discussions
- study your professor
- review your notes periodically

As finals week approaches, make a separate plan for that occasion. Start with the schedule for each test and then arrange the study times for each one. That usually means having to start the week before finals. On your plan, show the time for sleeping, which should be your usual seven to eight hours. Include times for meals, breaks, and some minor recreation to help with prolonged study times.

Tips for taking tests

Know what resources are available to the students in your high school or college. For instance, some professors will provide the class with copies of the Power Point presentations. Others may post online previous tests or sample questions for use in preparation. Make sure you attend review sessions, which are usually held the week before finals for all courses. Make sure you eat lightly just before a test and that you get your required amount of sleep.

When beginning to study, determine whether you are a morning or a night person. This information will tell you your most productive study time. Have available the tests that were returned to you during the semester or quarter. Review specifically the areas you missed, and bone up on that material. When studying for the exam, work by yourself first. Then, if possible, work with a small group to double-check your understanding while there is still time to do something about it.

Arrive at the testing site early to avoid any misunderstanding about the testing location. You will also have your choice of seats instead of having to take what is left over. Immediately go through your target outline/map, and if time permits, your major outline/map.

When in the testing situation, as obvious as it may seem, put your name and required information on the test and answer sheet. Go through the test quickly to allocate time for the entire test. Leave about ten minutes at the end to check your results. If something confuses you, ask for help. Don't pay any attention to what others might think. Settling your mind is far better than heading in a totally wrong direction.

Remember, you must start early to review notes and memorize material. Plan to use the distributed method of practice, which calls for spacing your learning sessions with breaks in between sessions, during which you will rest and relax or study a completely different subject.

Never do what is commonly called an all-nighter, if such can be avoided. It is devastating to your physical condition and will produce significant dampening effects on your test performance. Eliminate stress to whatever extent possible. Do not allow yourself to worry about anything during the critical testing session. Practice putting your worries into a compartment of your brain and closing the door. Promise yourself that you will worry about such things when finals are over. Keep in mind it is not the object of our worries that is the hindrance to us; it is our *view* of that worrisome object that does the damage. We are ultimately in charge of the outlook we hold. It all boils down to starting early, having good notes, doing the work, and keeping the appropriate attitude!

Chapter Summary

1. Preparation for finals begins on the first day of class.
2. Establish a plan that covers finals week and the week before.
3. Attend the review sessions.
4. Go through your master and trigger outlines/maps for each class.

28

Panty Raids for Fun and Profit

Or How to Learn Something in Spite of It All

Each spring, thousands of college seniors promenade majestically across hundreds of stages to press the Dean's sweaty palm with one hand while receiving that hard-won sheepskin (don't look too closely—it's paper) with the other. Flashbulbs explode. Audiences clap (they rarely applaud). Proud parents beam. Their son or daughter has "arrived."

Unfortunately, the pomp is often just so much circumstance. Beneath that scholarly veneer, it's disturbing to think just how little these freshly minted college grads really know. Oh, they've got the academic trivia memorized well enough to make a name for themselves on daytime television. However, when we get down to pragmatics, it is incredible how poorly adept they are at taking charge of a board meeting or even changing a tire.

This brings us to our final chapter. It's a peachy one, but if you have stayed on board this long, read on for a few more pages, and you can at least take credit for reading the whole book, if nothing more.

A big trouble with college today is that there is very little classroom time devoted to that kind of education we all need but rarely obtain. For four years, professors cram volumes of quotients, dates, theorems, systems, and formulas down our throats, most of it ending up on exams as pedagogic excrement. However, they fail to educate us in two equally, if not more important, areas of learning: They do not teach us leadership, and they do not teach us common sense. These you have to learn on your own.

Too familiar is the story of the business school graduate who understands perfectly the managerial grid, the double declining balance and the implications of the Hawthorne study, but when it comes to working through people to get things done, he or she might just as well fold up the tent.

This is why extracurricular activities are so important in the college student's overall growth, not just from the standpoint of emotional enjoyment but as part of the total learning experience.

The guy or gal who studies Business Administration must realize that running a business is, to a large extent, working with and through other people. A select few are blessed with this expertise at birth; to most, it is an art to be mastered through experience. The management student who sits for one hundred and thirty semester hours pouring over textbooks will likely be a poor manager. The science major who plans to teach physics will be less effective if he or she fails to understand and appreciate the multifaceted personalities who one day will make up his or her classroom. It is a rare occupation that does not require a certain talent for understanding and managing people.

The college campus provides a unique training ground for developing these leadership skills. College students are typically joiners, as evidenced by the scads of fraternities, sororities, social clubs, and student committees popping up all the time on the university scene. There exists an organization for every taste and interest. The Spelunker Club explores caves. The Geology Club digs for fossils. The Foreign Film Club promotes risqué movies; the Christian Leadership Club condemns them. These organizations are living laboratories wherein may be discovered one of life's great secrets—*The art of achievement results through interaction!*

Why then, with all the clubs and societies on today's campuses, doesn't everyone rise to the pinnacle of leadership?

The reason is simple. Each organization is made up of two groups: the Leaders and the Followers. As one might expect, the small percentage who are leaders in college later become the small percentage of leaders in the business world.

The leadership lessons to be learned are many—how to delegate authority, how much to expect from a committee, how to motivate others to best carry out their responsibilities, and so forth. Moreover, you don't have to be elected Exalted High Three-tailed Pasha in order to cultivate these principles. Even if you are only the chairman of the Scrapbook Committee, you can expect to benefit if you apply yourself with diligence and determination. It won't always be easy, of course. The trick is to enlist cooperation. And when the guys and gals would rather be down at the beer garden than painting the homecoming sign, delegation can be a problem.

Meanwhile, the guy or gal who perseveres through success or failure will learn some of life's most valuable lessons. Even the most Mickey Mouse organization (Student Government topic for today: Gum Chewing in the Auditorium) can be a conduit for leadership training. So long as you budget your time accordingly, this kind of education is hard to beat.

Not only do these organizations provide leadership skills, available nowhere else, they also offer first-class instruction in the good old art of Common Sense.

How many Phi Beta Kappas do we know with a string of plaudits as long as your graduation gown, but who are completely lost when faced with simple everyday tasks, such as filling out an income tax form or changing the oil in the crankcase? Send him or her to a formal dinner, and he or she mistakes the finger bowl for a soup dish. Let the air out of a tire on his or her car, and they are off to call AAA.

Spending four years working with others in similar predicaments provides wonderful therapy for these social cripples. Life in dorms, apartments, and frat/sorority houses has a way of polishing up the old personality.

For this reason, going away to school is a major part of the education process. The kids who live at home for four years are being cheated out of a large part of their education. If the family can't afford to send them, let them work their way through—or apply for one of the thousands of fellowships, scholarships, and federal grants which go begging every year.

Another way to add value to your education is through outside reading. Your campus bookstore is a goldmine of practical information not taught in regular classes. There are shelves of paperbacks whose subjects range from doing household electrical chores to buying a home. Books dealing with home medical treatments, watching football on television, shorthand, letter writing, and buying stocks and bonds, can only help to broaden one's utilitarian horizons through practical "How to" information rarely touched upon elsewhere. Financing a home, buying life insurance—how much more important to a young person starting out in life than who won the War of the Roses. The vocabulary-builder books are invaluable in boosting understanding and self-expression. Books by Dale Carnegie and Napoleon Hill have drastically changed lives, yet their cost is under a few bucks and reading time is just an hour or two.

Every college student should subscribe to at least one weekly news magazine or daily newspaper. The material taught in college courses will take on new meaning when related to the times in which we live. By keeping abreast of current events, then–now relationships will take root, even though you are not always consciously aware of that.

Finally, a student should become aware of the value of travel in contributing to one's overall education. With air travel cost comparatively low today and the many financial breaks available to students traveling abroad, you can spend as long as a month on the continent for under a thousand dollars. You will be surprised how those dull history, literature, government, and philosophy courses will come to life afterwards.

If you follow these suggestions, you should graduate from college with more than a piece of paper and a clammy handshake. When the handclaps have long faded, the dust settled on the college yearbook, and your freshman beanie is buried somewhere up in the attic, you will still continue to reap the bountiful fruits of academic labors many years removed —an education greatly desired, but rarely achieved.

End of sermon.

Chapter Summary

1. Classroom experiences provide only a part of your total education. Participation in extracurricular activities are of equal—often even greater— importance.

2. Leadership is learned by accepting responsibility, then working through other people to achieve the goals.

3. Tremendous values come from being on your own in a college environment away from home.

4. Outside practical reading results in widening the scope of your education.

5. The value of travel in supplementing and enhancing your regular studies should not be overlooked.

BIBLIOGRAPHY

Alliance for Excellent Education. 2006a. *Demography as Destiny: How America can Build a Better Future.* Washington, DC: AFEE.

Alliance for Excellent Education, Aug.2009. *The High Cost of High School Dropouts: What the Nation Pays for Inadequate High Schools.* Washington, DC: Author>

Archer, N. S. & R. Pippert (1962) "Don't Change the Answer! An exposé of the perennial myth that first choices are always the correct Ones." Clearing House. 37 39-41

Buzan. Tony. *Use Both Sides of Your Brain.* New York: Dutton, 1976

DeSalvo, L. *Writing As A Way of Healing: How Telling Our Stories Transforms Our Lives.* Boston: Beacon Press, 2000

Editorial Projects in Education (EPE). 2007. Diplomas count 2007: Ready for what? Preparing students for college, careers, and life after high school. Special issue, *Education Week* 26, no. 40: 40-41.

Foote, R. & C. Belinky, (1972) "It Pays To Switch? Consequences of Changing Answers on Multiple Choice Examinations." *Psychological Reports* 31, 667-673

Klein, K., and A. Boals. 2001 "Expressive Writing Can Increase Working Memory" Cape City: *Journal of Experimental Psychology: General* 130: 520-533

Kruger, Justin, Dale T. Miller, and Derrick Wirtz. "Counterfactual Thinking and the First Instinct Fallacy." *Journal of Personality and Social Psychology*, May 2005 Vol. 88 Number 5 pages 725-735. American Psychological Association

Miller, Julie. *Business Writing that Counts*. Book Publishers Network.

Pennebaker. J. W. *Writing To Heal: A Guided Journal For Recovering From Trauma and Emotional Upheaval*. New Harbinger Publications, Inc., 2004

Pennebaker, J. W. *Opening Up: The Healing Power of Expressing Emotions*. New York: Guilford, 1997

Swindoll, Charles R. *Strengthening Your Grip*, Nashville: W. Publishing Group, 1982, 206-207.

APPENDIX 1

"Counterfactual Thinking and the First-Instinct Fallacy"

Kruger, Wirtz and Miller

eported in *The Journal of Personality and Social Psychology* Volume 88, No. 5, 725-735 ©2005 by the American Psychological Association, reprinted with permission.

These results were obtained from 1,561 University of Illinois students, 49 percent men, 51 percent women, who took the introductory psychology course, fall 2000, PSYCH 100 multiple-choice midterm exam.

The tables following show the actual/predicted results of students who changed 3,291 answers. The answer changes from WRONG to RGHT outnumbered by a margin of two to one the answer changes from RIGHT to WRONG. Another study of the test item changes from tests administered the previous year resulted in essentially the same two-to-one margin in favor of those who changed wrong to right.

Table 1

Predicted and actual proportion of answer changes from WRONG to RIGHT, RIGHT to WRONG, and WRONG to WRONG

Answer change	Predicted %	Actual %
Wrong to Right	33	51
Right to Wrong	42	25
Wrong to Wrong	24	23

Table 2

Predicted and actual proportion of individuals who changed one or more answers that were: Helped by Answer Switching, Hurt by Switching, or Neither.

Results of Switching	Predicted %	Actual %
Helped by Switching	33	54
Hurt by Switching	38	19
Neither	29	27

Note that the predicted percentages in the Tables above provide further evidence of the First-Instinct Fallacy. The third row (wrong to wrong and neither) in the above tables was not applicable.

APPENDIX 2
Examples of Test Items

True/False

T or F There is a negative correlation between level of education and earnings potential.

T or F The single most significant decision you can make on a day-to-day basis is the choice of attitude.

T or F The best way to study for class is while lying in bed.

T or F The Greek system is strictly a social club.

T or F Expressive writing can only be used effectively with minor emotional upheavals.

Multiple Choice

1. When selecting a major it is best to:

    (a) Talk to those who know you well.

    (b) Take psychological tests.

    (c) Visit a person who works in your field of interest.

(d) Sleep on your decision.

(e) All of the above.

2. When doing public speaking:

(a) Try not to look at your audience.

(b) Prepare at the last moment.

(c) If you are not sure, mumble.

(d) Don't speak loudly, it may wake someone.

(e) None of the above.

3. What number of high school students fail to graduate each year?

(a) 13,200,000

(b) 1,230,000

(c) 1,320,000

(d) 132,000

4. What is the number of freshmen entering high school each year?

(a) 40,000

(b) 400,000

(c) 4,000,000

(d) 40,000,000

5. Which of the alternatives should you avoid when getting an education?

(a) Joining the military

(b) Using the Community College system

(c) Attending a trade school

(d) Attending the university

(e) Joining OLK and EBB

APPENDIX

Fill in the Blank

1. The critical aspect about our attitude is that life is truly _____% what happens to me, and _____% how I respond to it.

2. The favorite implement of torture at exam time is the _____ exam.

3. Immediately after highlighting a chapter you should _____ or _____ the material.

4. The trigger outline should contain _____ or _____ to facilitate memorization.

5. If you cut a class you should _____ the professor and _____ the material.

Matching

1. Match the job with the appropriate education option.

(1.) Colonel		(a) Hard knocks
(2.) Plumber		(b) College
(3.) Accountant		(c) Military
(4.) Factory worker		(d) High School
(5.) Entrepreneur		(e) Trade school

2. Match the make with the model.

(1.) Jeep	(a) Tahoe
(2.) Ford	(b) Camry
(3.) Chevy	(c) Wrangler
(4.) Toyota	(d) Continental
(5.) Nissan	(e) Fleetwood
(6.) Cadillac	(f) Exterra
(7.) Lincoln	(g) Taurus

3. Match the team with the sport.

(1.) Cowboys   (a) Basketball
(2.) Mavericks   (b) Hockey
(3) Rangers   (c) Football
(4.) Desperados   (d) Baseball
(5.) Stars   (e) Arena football

4. Match the States with their Capitals.

(1.) Texas   (a) Phoenix
(2.) Louisiana   (b) Lincoln
(3.) California   (c) Indianapolis
(4.) Arizona   (d) Austin
(5.) Nebraska   (e) Sacramento
(6.) Indiana   (f) Baton Rouge

5. Match the author with their book

(1.) John Steinbeck   (a) Harry Potter
(2.) J.D. Salinger   (b) Winning
(3.) Hunter S. Thompson (c) Grapes of Wrath
(4.) Jack Welch   (d) Catcher in the Rye
(5.) J. K. Rowling   (e) Fear and Loathing

Essay questions

1. Compare and contrast the political process in the United States and Canada.
2. Describe the resulting relationships from the North American Free Trade Agreement.
3. Explain the key aspects of the Taft-Hartley Act.
4. Interpret the foreign policy of Austria and Germany.
5. Extrapolate the outcomes resulting from China's birth restrictions.

Answers:

True/False Questions

1. False
2. True
3. False
4. False
5. False

Multiple-choice Questions

1. (e) All of the above
2. (e) None of the above
3. (b) 1,230,000
4. (c) 4,000,000
5. (e) Joining OLK and EBB

Fill in the blank Questions

1. **10%** what happens to me, and **90%** how I respond to it.
2. The **essay** exam.
3. You should **outline** or **idea map** the material.
4. Should contain **stick figures, jargon** or **pictures, colors** to facilitate memorization.
5. Should **meet with** the professor and **make up** the material.

Matching Questions

1. 1. (c) Military
   2. (e) Trade School
   3. (b) College
   4. (d) High School
   5. (a) Hard Knocks

2. 1. (c) Wrangler
   2. (g) Taurus
   3. (a) Tahoe
   4. (b) Camry
   5. (f) Exterra
   6. (e) Fleetwood
   7. (d) Continental

3. 1. (c) Football
   2. (a) Basketball
   3. (d) Baseball
   4. (e) Arena Football
   5. (b) Hockey

4. 1. (d) Austin
   2. (f) Baton Rouge
   3. (e) Sacramento
   4. (a) Phoenix
   5. (b) Lincoln
   6. (c) Indianapolis

5. 1. (c) Grapes of Wrath
   2. (d) Catcher in the Rye
   3. (e) Fear and Loathing
   4. (b) Winning
   5. (a) Harry Potter

About the Authors

Dr. Donald L. Wass

Donald L.Wass earned his PhD in psychology from Purdue University. His master's and undergraduate degrees in psychology were awarded at Western Michigan University. He has had thirty years of experience lecturing worldwide on such topics as: Managing Management Time, motivation, stress management, and team development. He coauthored, with William Oncken Jr., the article "Management Time—Who's Got the Monkey?," published in the *Harvard Business Review*. The article was named an HBR classic, and was listed as one of the two most influential, best-selling HBR reprints. Dr. Wass is president of the William Oncken Company of Texas, a provider of management seminars; and CEO of TEC Texas DFW, an organization dedicated to increasing the effectiveness and enhancing the lives of CEO's.

Contact Information:

Donald L. Wass Ph.D
923 Creekdale Drive
Richardson, Texas 75080
Office: (972) 238-9382
Home: (972) 231-1586
E-mail: tectexas@aol.com

Donald L. Wass Jr.

Don Wass Jr. has been a highly motivated professional with over twenty successful years in sales, sales management, education, finance, and real estate. He served as Director of Recruitment and Director of Education at Professional Court Reporting School in Richardson, Texas. His experience includes National Sales Manager for Homestore.com, Arizona Builders, 1-800-HOUSING, and the Moore Companies. He worked in the financial arena with Merrill Lynch and was owner and president of JTS in Dallas, Texas. He currently helps business owners and prospective owners realize their dreams with Crest Commercial Real Estate. His professional licenses include the Series 7, Series 66, insurance, mortgage loan officer and commercial real estate. Don received his BA in Psychology from Southern Methodist University in Dallas, Texas, and completed extensive master's work in Psychology from East Texas State University. He is married with three children and currently resides in Richardson, Texas.

Contact Information:

Donald L. Wass Jr.
Phone: (972) 400-2905
E-mail: dwass@crestcommercial.com

Amanda Rose Ray

Amanda Rose Ray is currently a college student pursuing a BA in Psychology and aiming to attend medical school to specialize in neurology. She graduated from Bishop Lynch High School. At the age of seventeen, she wrote and had published her first novel, *Ambivalence*.

Amanda Rose attended the University of Central Florida for two years, during which time she contributed articles to *Florida Golf Central Magazine*, where she also worked as a production assistant. She transferred to the University of North Texas to complete her degree in psychology and to fulfill her premed requirements. She currently resides in Denton, Texas.

Contact Information:

Amanda "Rose" Ray
923 Creekdale Drive
Richardson, Texas 75080
Email: catchermach5@aol.com